10779596 10.90

THE
FOREIGN
POLICY
DEBATE

STEPHEN GOODE

THE FOREIGN POLICY DEBATE

HUMAN RIGHTS AND AMERICAN FOREIGN POLICY

Franklin Watts   An Impact Book
New York ▪ London ▪ Toronto ▪ Sydney ▪ 1984

Library of Congress Cataloging in Publication Data

Goode, Stephen.
The foreign policy debate.

(An Impact book)
Bilbiography: p.
Includes index.
Summary: Examines the abuse of human rights in
today's world and discusses the controversial role
of American foreign policy in relation to this issue.
1. United States—Foreign relations—
1945-   Juvenile literature.
2. Civil rights (International law)—
Juvenile literature.   [1. United States
—Foreign relations—1945-   2.
Civil rights (International law)]   I Title.
E840.G64 1984   323.4   84-10384
ISBN 0-531-04753-9

CONTENTS

THE
FOREIGN
POLICY
DEBATE

PREFACE

All human beings are born free and equal in dignity and rights. They are endowed with reason and conscience and should act towards one another in a spirit of brotherhood.

Article 1 of the United Nations
Universal Declaration of Human Rights

Item. Kampuchea (formerly Cambodia). In April 1975 a communist government came to power in this Southeast Asian country. Over the next four years, it undertook a vast program of reform designed to uproot the past and remold Cambodian society.

Millions were compelled to move from the cities to the countryside to work in "forced labor" battalions. The laborers toiled long hours and were allowed little food. Untold numbers died.

In addition, government troops killed an estimated *one million* Cambodians regarded as "enemies" of the new regime. Among those killed were Buddhists who refused to abandon traditional religious observances and the sick and "lazy," who did not work sufficiently hard to please the new government.

Many observers believe that as many as *three million* Cambodians (out of a population of seven million) died as a result of the executions and the harshness of the government's reform programs.

Item. Amnesty International, an independent human-rights agency located in London, England, reports that government repression is on the rise in the world today and that *serious* human-rights violations occur in over one hundred nations.

According to the agency, torture of political prisoners has rapidly increased since World War II and has now become very sophisticated. Thanks to modern technology, government police can now break a prisoner's will without leaving a mark on his or her body.

Among the methods of torture Amnesty International found in use were the "grill," the "Parrot's Perch," and the "Wet Submarine." The grill is a metal frame on which a prisoner is stretched out and repeatedly shocked. The Parrot's Perch is a bar from which the prisoner is hung by the knees, hands and feet tied together, while the body receives electric shocks. In the Wet Submarine, the prisoner is repeatedly immersed to the point of drowning in water or urine.

Amnesty International also reports that sexual tortures are frequent. They include the rape of women by trained dogs, the insertion of rats into female sexual organs, and the suspension of bricks from men's testicles.

Item. It is estimated that throughout the world ten million people die each year from starvation. Untold millions of others are so undernourished from birth that they suffer throughout life from the physical and mental effects of malnutrition.

Most of the world's people are poor and illiterate, and most do not have access to an education that might improve their lives. Most, likewise, do not have access to adequate health care or to adequate clothing and housing.

Experts fear that the cycle of poverty and ignorance is likely to continue far into the future. Recent U.N. statistics show that the gap between the rich and poor nations is increasing. Moreover, the same statistics show that the gap between the poverty-stricken people and the rich of the world's poorest nations is also on the increase. Everywhere the plight of the poor increases while the comfort of the rich grows.

The three "items" above describe three different kinds of human-rights abuse. Each—the hunger and poverty of millions, the widespread torture of political prisoners, and the mass executions in Kampuchea—is deeply disturbing. They did not happen in the distant and barbaric past where they could be excused and forgotten. They occurred only recently and are continuing to take place right now.

This book will look at the problem of human-rights abuse in the world today. It will also look at the problem of human-rights issues and American foreign policy. Should the United States use its enormous power, wealth, and influence to improve the condition of human rights abroad, as many Americans have urged? Or should America recognize that it can do little to alleviate human-rights abuse in foreign lands and concentrate on more traditional—and attainable—foreign-policy goals, as others have claimed, such as arms control and trade agreements?

There are strong arguments on both sides of the issue, and we shall look at them. Chapter 1, "Understanding Human Rights and Foreign Policy," will answer questions like "What are human rights?" and "What are the pros and cons of an active human-rights policy?"

Chapter 2 will turn to the U.S. Congress during the 1970s, when a number of senators and representatives began to insist that human-rights goals be joined to American foreign policy in an effort to improve human-rights performance abroad.

Chapter 3, "Jimmy Carter and Human Rights," will look at the administration of President Carter (1977–1981). Carter was a strong human-rights advocate and made human rights the centerpiece of his foreign policy.

Chapter 4 discusses the administration of President Ronald Reagan, who took office in 1981. Reagan has abandoned Carter's emphasis on human rights and has chosen to pursue a foreign policy that seeks to gain respect abroad for America's power and military might.

Chapter 5 looks at the role human-rights issues have played in American history. We will find that many Americans in the past have been strong human-rights advocates while others have argued that the United States should not concern itself with the private and internal affairs of other nations in order to improve their behavior.

Chapters 6, 7, and 8 look at South Africa, South Korea, and the Soviet Union, three nations with very different backgrounds but with long records of human-rights abuse. America's relationship with each of these countries has been complex and has involved difficult and formidable problems of human rights and foreign policy.

Chapter 9 discusses two international agencies—the United Nations and the Organization of American States—that offer the United States an opportunity to work in concert with other nations for the improvement of human rights. Chapter 10 will offer a few conclusions about human rights and foreign policy.

What this book hopes to convey to the reader is an understanding of the importance of the human-rights issue in today's
world. It also hopes to convey the fact that the human-rights
issue is complex and offers no easy solutions or answers.

There are many good reasons why America should seek to
improve human rights abroad through its foreign policy, and
there are many ways that human-rights issues can be made a
part of foreign policy.

But there are many equally good reasons that argue against
mixing human-rights issues and American foreign policy. This
book will explore these issues and problems.

CHAPTER
1
UNDERSTANDING HUMAN RIGHTS AND FOREIGN POLICY

Human rights is the genuine, historical inevitability of our times. . . . the central form in which mankind is expressing its new political awakening.
. . .

Zbigniew Brzezinski
President Carter's national
security adviser, in 1978

There is a worldwide growing abuse of human rights, with violations of international standards so widespread that we are, indeed, facing a global human rights crisis.

Former Representative
Donald Fraser in 1977

Human rights may be divided into two general categories. The first is civil and political rights. The second includes what have been called social and economic rights. The two groups have very basic differences.

The first category, *civil and political rights*, are the rights most familiar to Americans. They include the rights to "life, liberty, and the pursuit of happiness" mentioned in the Declaration of Independence of 1776.

They likewise include the rights and freedoms listed in the Bill of Rights, the first ten amendments to the American Constitution. The Bill of Rights guarantees freedom of speech and of assembly, freedom of the press, and freedom of religion. It guarantees that "the right of the people to be secure in their persons, houses, and effects, against unreasonable searches and seizures, shall not be violated, . . ." and promises every American the right to a "speedy trial" by an impartial jury when accused of a crime.

One of the most significant provisions of the Bill of Rights declares that Americans cannot "be deprived of life, liberty, or property, without due process of law. . . ." Another states that "cruel and unusual punishments" cannot be inflicted upon American citizens.

What these kinds of rights are designed to do is to free the individual from *government repression.* They do this by limiting the power and authority of the government over the lives of every citizen and by giving each citizen the right to challenge the government of his or her rights are violated.

In America, for example, citizens cannot, by law, be arrested and tortured if their political views differ from those of the government in power. The Constitution and American law are meant to protect every individual from government harassment and intimidation.

But there is also a second, more positive, side to civil and political rights, and this is the guarantee that every person in a democracy has the right to participate in the process of government. The American Constitution grants Americans the right to vote and to hold public office. American democracy is based on the belief that a government should be responsive to the opinions and demands of its citizens.

Civil and political rights have a long history. They have not only been embodied in the Declaration of Independence and the Constitution, but also in documents such as the Magna Carta of 1215, the English Petition of Right of 1628, the English Bill of Rights of 1689, and the French Declaration of the Rights of Man and of the Citizen of 1789. Today civil and political rights find their clearest manifestation and most ardent defenders in the United States, Australia, New Zealand, Canada, the United Kingdom and France, and the nations of Western Europe.

Since World War II, Japan has also developed democratic institutions that protect civil and political rights. In the majority of nations in today's world, however, civil and political rights are not guaranteed and there are few laws that protect individuals from government intimidation or repression.

The second category of human rights are *social and economic rights*. These rights include the right to a job and to an education. They likewise include freedom from poverty and hunger, and the rights to proper medical care and proper nutrition.

Social and economic rights do not seek to limit or restrain government power. On the contrary, they call upon government to help provide jobs and opportunities for education, medical care, and food needed by the poor and underprivileged.

Social and economic rights also have a long history. European revolutionaries in the nineteenth century insisted on their significance and called upon government to provide basic human social and economic needs.

The citizen's right to a job and to government assistance was mentioned in the Mexican Constitution of 1917, in the German Constitution of 1919, and the Constitution of the Republic of Spain in 1931. The constitutions of the Soviet Union and of other communist nations likewise guarantee the social and economic rights of their citizens.

But social and economic rights are a controversial issue. Many Americans, for example, believe that civil and political rights are the most basic human rights, and the only rights that can truly be protected by government. Social and economic rights—the right to a job, to an education, and so on—they regard as problems that must be solved by individual initiative and hard work and not by government action.

Defenders of social and economic rights, however, are of another opinion. They believe that social and economic rights are the most basic human rights and that once a government has answered the social and economic needs of its people, it can then turn its attention to other matters, such as political and social rights.

One articulate defender of the importance of social and economic rights is Eddison Zvobgo, a lawyer and citizen of Zimbabwe, a developing nation in southern Africa. Zvobgo believes that the primary problem facing poor nations is the solution of long-term evils such as malnutrition, illiteracy, and disease. For Zvobgo, it is more important that poor nations arrange for their people to be adequately fed than that they grant them freedom of speech or press. It is likewise more important that the poor peoples of the world have jobs and proper medical care than that they have the right to vote.

Zvobgo does not deny the attractiveness and significance of Western-style political and civil freedoms. He hopes that these freedoms will come some day to Zimbabwe and other third-world nations. In the meantime, he believes, that third-world nations must strive to alter age-old habits of mind and ways of living that prevent change and improvement. The only way to alter these habits of mind, he argues, is by putting an end to poverty and illiteracy and providing the opportunity for education.

To reach these goals, Zvobgo concludes, third-world governments must sometimes be repressive and heavy-handed. Weak governments, he explains, could never tackle and resolve the immense social and economic problems faced by the third world. Only strong, decisive governments will have the power and authority necessary to break the cycle of poverty and ignorance that plagues poor nations.

Zvobgo is impatient with those who claim that third-world nations should adopt democracy and guarantee political and civil rights. Even in the United States and Western Europe, he points out, democratic institutions are only about two hundred years old.

Before democracy appeared, he notes, Western nations were governed by absolute monarchs or ruling elites, while the vast majority of people were powerless, poor, and without rights. Since democracy took a long time to develop in the West, Zvobgo concludes, Western Europeans and Americans should be more patient with the development of democratic institutions in third-world countries.

Zvobgo makes one point that even the most ardent advocate of civil and political rights must agree with. The final goal of human rights, he believes, is the creation and preservation of human worth and dignity. Poverty and ignorance, he says, degrade individuals and keep them from achieving their full human stature. Similarly, the advocate of political and social rights believes that without freedom of expression, of worship, and other like rights, human life cannot be full and complete. It is the search for human worth and dignity that unites the advocates of human rights, whether they stress the importance of social and economic rights, of political and civil rights, or a combination of both categories. And it is this search for human dignity that makes human rights the important issue it is in the world of today.

Human Rights and Foreign Policy:
Pros and Cons

Foreign policy, like politics, can be defined as the pursuit of the possible through the application of power and persuasion. It is a means that nations use to settle minor disputes and even major disagreements among themselves short of war and the use of force. Traditionally, human rights have not been regarded as a subject suited to foreign policy and international arbitration.

Human-rights advocates today, however, cite a number of compelling reasons why the United States should include human-rights issues on its foreign-policy agenda. One of the most compelling reasons is that Americans cannot turn their backs on human rights because it is a long-established American tradition to be concerned about injustice wherever it occurs.

Since the founding of the American republic in 1776, human-rights advocates tell us, Americans have hoped that their style of freedom and liberty could be established elsewhere in the world. Americans have traditionally despised repressive governments that violate human rights and have cheered foreign champions of human rights and liberty. It is this freedom-loving tradition, human-rights advocates claim, that should cause Americans to support the human-rights movement throughout the world.

A second reason for the inclusion of human-rights issues in American foreign policy is that the United States has an international *obligation* to support and encourage human rights abroad. Human-rights advocates point out that America has signed several treaties that require it to take a stand against human-rights abuse in foreign lands. To ignore this commitment, they say, would be to violate an agreement the United States had solemnly promised to obey.

One commitment that obliges the United States to respect the cause of human rights is the U.N. Universal Declaration of Human Rights, which America signed in 1948. The Universal Declaration announced that basic human rights—including social and economic rights and well as civil and political rights—were "a common standard of achievement for all peoples and all nations." It called upon "every individual and every organ of society" to "strive by teaching and education to promote respect for these rights and freedoms, and by progressive measures, national and international, to secure their universal and effective recognition and observance. . . ."

A second commitment that requires American support for human rights abroad is the Helsinki Final Act, which the United States signed in 1975 along with thirty-four other nations, including the Soviet Union, Canada, and the nations of Eastern and Western Europe. The Helsinki Final Act obliges the thirty-five "participating states" to "promote and encourage the effective exercise of civil, political, economic, social, cultural and other rights and freedoms" and to "constantly respect these rights and freedoms in their mutual relations." It likewise obliges them to "endeavor jointly and separately . . . to promote universal and effective respect" for human rights "because these rights are essential to peace, justice, and continuing friendly relations" among the nations of the world. By signing documents like these, the human-rights advocates claim, the United States has clearly promised to seek a more just and better world—and to work to put a stop to human-rights abuse whenever and wherever it takes place.

Finally, human-rights advocates urge the United States to make human-rights issues a part of foreign policy because it is in the American national interest to do so. For too long, they maintain, America has been viewed worldwide as a powerful, wealthy, and aggressive nation that has little interest in the problems faced by other countries. A serious human-rights effort on the part of the United States, the advocates of human rights say, could change this negative image into a more positive one. America could become the champion of human freedom and dignity and the enemy of repression and human degradation. Peoples that once regarded the United States as an enemy would then become its friends. Those that regarded it with suspicion and distrust could be persuaded to shed that suspicion and distrust.

The arguments in favor of an active human-rights policy are strong and persuasive, and appeal to American idealism. But there are also strong and persuasive arguments that urge a prudent and limited position on human-rights issues, especially when they are mixed with foreign policy. Few Americans, if any, would argue that their country should take no position on human rights. But many would argue that any mixture of human rights and foreign policy undertaken by the United States should be carefully considered and thought out before it is put into action.

Those who argue for a carefully considered human-rights policy should not be regarded as opponents of human rights or enemies of human freedom and dignity. They can more correctly be seen as men and women who recognize that even the best and most idealistic of human intentions can go awry and produce more evil than good.

Those who urge caution in human rights ask us first to consider realistically how much America is capable of doing. The variety and frequency of human-rights violations in the world today, they point out, are overwhelming and on the increase. The majority of present-day governments are repressive. Many governments—including some of our most loyal and valued allies—torture political dissidents and jail citizens for purely political reasons. Freedom of speech, press, and religion exist only in a small number of nations. The problems of hunger, poverty, illiteracy, joblessness, and disease are so widespread that they defy solution.

Faced with the enormous size of the human-rights problem, the critics ask, is it reasonable to ask the United States to take on a problem so large and unmanageable? Wouldn't it be better for America to limit its foreign-policy goals to what is practicable and achievable rather than face the frustration that would come with the failure to attain unreasonable and distant goals, such as the improvement of human rights abroad?

Second, those who question the wisdom of an active human-rights policy point out that the United States has no business telling other governments how to behave. It may be true, they say, that America's commitment to agreements such as the Universal Declaration on Human Rights and the Helsinki Final Act obliges the United States to work for the advancement of human rights. But it is equally true, they add, that America has signed agreements promising never to interfere or to intervene in the private and domestic affairs of other nations. The United Nations Charter, signed by the United States in 1945, contains a provision that pledges that one member nation will not involve itself in the internal matters of another member nation. The Helsinki Final Act contains a similar provision pledging noninterference.

Moreover, the critics argue, the principle of nonintervention in the affairs of other nations is an old and trusted one that has guided relations among the governments of the world for centuries and should remain a central premise of American foreign policy. Because the U.S. does not welcome criticism or intervention from abroad in its own domestic affairs, so it should not take the opportunity to criticize or intervene in foreign countries when other nations pursue policies disagreeable to America.

Finally, the critics of an active human-rights policy maintain that such a policy is not in America's best national interest. They ask us to consider what the results of a worldwide campaign for human rights might be. If the United States criticizes friendly nations such as South Korea or the Philippines, which have long records of human-rights abuse, it runs the risk of alienating longtime allies. Should America run the risk of losing loyal friends, merely for the sake of a human-rights policy?

If America attacks the Soviet Union for human-rights violations, it may anger Soviet leaders and undermine what little understanding exists between the world's two superpowers. Shouldn't the United States remain silent about Soviet human-rights abuse, so that America and the U.S.S.R. can achieve agreements on other important issues, such as arms limitation and the control of nuclear weapons?

If the United States points to the poor human-rights record of third-world nations, it is accused of arrogance and loses what influence it may have among the poor and developing regions of the world. Since the United States has much to lose and little to gain from a vigorous human-rights policy, the critics conclude, it is best to play down the human-rights issue. We live in an imperfect and often brutal world, they add, and cannot expect men and women to behave like angels or imperfect societies to improve at America's command.

Clearly, there are strong arguments on both sides of the human-rights issue. But whatever position one takes, the importance of human rights in today's world cannot be denied.

A majority of the world's governments are repressive, and most fail to guarantee human rights of any kind. A majority of the world's people are ill fed, ill clothed, ill housed, poorly educated, and unable to receive proper medical care. Only a minority of governments protect free speech, free press, freedom of religion, and other similar rights.

The human-rights issue is important because it concerns the kind of image the United States wants to reflect abroad and the kind of influence it wants to have in world affairs. Because the United States is powerful and wealthy, the position it takes on human rights is of enormous significance and can affect the world for good or for ill.

But the debate over human rights is not simply a question of "for" and "against." It is a question of *which* human rights should be emphasized and *how* foreign policy can be used to obtain human rights abroad. It is also a question of *what degree* of influence America should exert and of *where* and *at what times* that influence should come into play. In the following chapters, we shall see how Americans have made human-rights issues a part of American foreign policy in the recent past and how human-rights issues are likely to continue to play a part in future American foreign policy.

CHAPTER

2

THE U.S. CONGRESS ADDRESSES HUMAN RIGHTS

. . . we all want the world to know that if the United States stands for anything in the world, it stands for upholding basic human rights."

Congressman
Tom Harkin, 1975

The question is, will we, by our positive efforts, help to affect and move this global upheaval in a direction consistent with our values and beliefs? Or will we merely resist it? Will we design our future or will we simply resign ourselves to it?

The late Senator
Hubert Humphrey, 1978

In the early 1970s, Representative Donald Fraser, a liberal Democrat from Minnesota, began to devote his considerable energy and enthusiasm to the cause of human rights. His example was taken up by other representatives and senators, and soon Congress was passing bills that tied human-rights issues to American foreign policy. Human rights, it seemed, was an idea whose time had come.

Fraser's concern about human rights had been awakened during the American civil rights movement of the 1950s and 1960s. One of the finest bills Congress had passed in recent years, he believed, was the Civil Rights Act of 1964, which had guaranteed equality under the law to black Americans. If Congress could address the problems of America's repressed minorities, he reasoned, could it not also turn its attention to the repressed and underprivileged abroad?

But the primary reason that Fraser and other like-minded members of Congress turned to human rights was a deep dissatisfaction with the foreign policy of the Nixon administration. President Nixon and his national security adviser and later secretary of state, Henry Kissinger, they believed, supported repressive governments abroad and ignored the enormous human suffering these governments caused.

U.S. support for repressive regimes, Fraser argued, damaged America's image. The United States, he maintained, should be in the business of fostering freedom and liberty in foreign lands, not suffering and repression. He hoped that Congress might work to alter and improve American foreign policy.

Fraser was a member of the House Committee on Foreign Affairs and chairman of the Subcommittee on International Organizations and Movements. In 1973 his subcommittee began to hold hearings on human-rights issues. Human-rights experts testified before the subcommittee, as did numerous victims of human-rights abuse. Fraser wanted the hearings to be as thorough as possible.

In 1974 the subcommittee published its findings in a report entitled *Human Rights in the World Community: A Call for U.S. Leadership*. The report called for a vigorous American commitment to improve the state of human rights throughout the world. "The human rights factor is not accorded the high priority it deserves in our country's foreign policy," the report declared. "Too often," it continued, the human-rights issue "becomes invisible on the vast foreign policy horizon."

The report concluded with a statement on the importance of human rights in the world today. "An increasingly interdependent world," it said, "means that disregard for human rights in one country can have repercussions in others." For Americans, it added, a "higher priority for human rights in foreign policy is both morally imperative and practically necessary."

The report listed twenty-nine recommendations to help increase the priority of human rights in foreign-policy making. One recommendation urged Congress to pass bills cutting off financial aid to nations with records of human-rights abuse. Another called for the reorganization of the State Department to assure that human-rights issues were given proper hearing in that department's activities.

The publication of the subcommittee's report did not quell Representative Fraser's interest in human rights. His subcommittee continued to hold hearings on human rights until 1978 for a total of over 150 hearings in over 40 countries with records of human-rights abuse. The results of these hearings were published in additional subcommittee reports.

Fraser received strong support from Washington's numerous human-rights lobbies. Independent organizations such as the International League for Human Rights and Amnesty International sent lobbyists to Capitol Hill to advise members of Congress on human-rights abuse and urge passage of human-rights legislation. Other lobbying groups also stepped up pressure on Congress to take notice of human-rights issues. Among the most significant of these groups were the National Council of Churches, B'nai B'rith International, the AFL-CIO, and the Federation of American Scientists.

Congress responded with a number of bills designed to enhance human rights abroad. These bills took two forms. Some were general in scope and were directed against any country with a poor record on human rights. Others were directed against specifically named countries with long histories of severe human-rights violations.

An example of a bill that was general in scope was the Foreign Assistance Act of 1973. In this piece of legislation, Congress declared that "it is the sense of Congress that the President should deny any economic or military assistance to the government of any foreign country which practices internment or imprisonment of that country's citizens for political purposes."

The bill, however, lacked teeth. Because it stated only the "sense"—or intention—of Congress, it was not binding on the president, who could continue handing out economic or military assistance at his own discretion. Nevertheless, Congress, for the first time, had gone on record as opposing aid to countries that practiced the imprisonment of political dissidents.

Two years later, Congress passed a stronger piece of legislation: Section 310 of the International Development and Food Assistance Act of 1975. Also known as the "Harkin amendment" for its sponsor, Representative Tom Harkin (Democrat, Iowa), this bill stated that it was the sense of Congress that assistance should be withheld from any nation violating human rights.

But the Harkin amendment added two new provisions. First, if the president decided to give assistance to nations with known records of human-rights abuse, he was required to submit a written statement to Congress explaining how that assistance would *directly* benefit the people of that nation. Second, if Congress disagreed with the president's written statement, it could withhold assistance to that country by a concurrent vote of both the House of Representatives and the Senate.

The Harkin amendment was one of the strongest human-rights bills passed by Congress. Between 1976 and 1979, further congressional legislation directed agencies such as the Inter-American Development Bank and the African Development Fund to take human-rights violations into consideration when granting loans to foreign nations.

The second type of human-rights legislation passed by Congress in the 1970s was directed at specific nations. Argentina, Chile, and Uruguay were selected for reprimand, as were the Soviet Union, Uganda, and a number of other nations.

Congress singled out Chile in 1974, Uruguay in 1976, and

Argentina in 1978 because the military dictatorships that governed each of these countries were brutally repressive and involved in the imprisonment, torture, and murder of political dissidents. Strong curbs were placed on military and financial assistance to Chile, while arms shipments and military aid to Argentina and Uruguay were cut off completely.

The Jackson-Vanik amendment, passed by Congress in 1974, was directed against the Soviet Union and sought to punish the U.S.S.R. for the severe restrictions it placed on Soviet Jews who wished to obtain passports to leave the country. The amendment declared that Soviet-American trade agreements would not receive congressional approval unless the Soviet Union abolished its severe passport restrictions and allowed Soviet Jews greater freedom of travel and emigration.

A 1978 bill was directed against the government of President Idi Amin of Uganda. Amin had come to power in 1971 and had used his position to order the slaughter of more than 300,000 Ugandans he regarded as opponents of his rule. The bill placed a trade embargo on coffee from Uganda, the country's only important cash crop. The embargo was lifted in 1979, after Amin had been driven from power.

How successful was the campaign for human rights undertaken by Congress in the 1970s? If the primary goal of the campaign was to improve the practice of human rights abroad, the answer can only be that it was not at all successful.

The Soviet Union deeply resented the Jackson-Vanik amendment and lifted none of the restrictions on Jewish emigration from the U.S.S.R. Soviet leaders angrily declared that Soviet domestic policy would not be dictated by the U.S. Congress and denounced what they called unjustified interference by a foreign nation in Soviet internal affairs.

The coffee embargo directed against Idi Amin came too late to have any real effect on his dictatorship. The bills directed against Argentina, Chile, and Uruguay aroused only anger and resentment in those countries and did nothing to improve the cause of human rights.

The Harkin amendment and other similar bills that declared the "sense" of Congress in favor of human rights lacked the strength and bite necessary to be effective instruments of human-rights policy. However, the congressional campaign for human rights should not be regarded as a complete failure. The campaign did put Congress on record, for the whole world to see, as a proponent of human rights, and it did lead to several significant changes.

The most important of those changes occurred in the State Department. In 1973, when Representative Donald Fraser first began to hold hearings on human rights, Secretary of State Henry Kissinger privately referred to the congressman as a "madman." It was not in the best interests of the nation, Kissinger told his aides, for Congress to become involved in foreign policy. The results, he said, could only be "random" and "unpredictable"— and therefore undesirable.

Kissinger believed that human-rights issues could best be served through "quiet diplomacy," where complaints about human-rights abuse were made to foreign nations privately and in secret. Bills passed by Congress were too open and public, he argued, to be effective diplomacy.

Kissinger never abandoned his personal belief that human rights were not a fit subject for foreign policy. But he did give in to congressional demands that the State Department show greater respect for human-rights issues. In Lusaka, Zambia, in April 1976, for example, he denounced racism and declared that an end to racism in southern Africa was "the moral imperative" of our time. "Justice," he said, "can command by the force of its rightness, instead of by force of arms."

At the meeting of the General Assembly of the Organization of American States (O.A.S.) in Santiago, Chile, later the same year, Kissinger announced that "the condition of human rights as assessed by the OAS Human Rights Commission has impaired our relationship with Chile and will continue to do so." The generals who made up Chile's military dictatorship were present when Kissinger spoke. Kissinger later told the generals that he personally might favor more aid to Chile, but that Congress was strongly against that aid and would vote it down.

The State Department under Kissinger began to reorganize itself to deal more effectively with human-rights issues. On April 4, 1974, the department ordered U.S. embassies in sixty-eight countries to issue reports on the condition of human rights in the nation where each embassy was located. Each of the sixty-eight nations were countries that received American aid and assistance.

The next year, 1975, the State Department organized the Bureau of Human Rights and Humanitarian Affairs to deal with human rights. The department also assigned a human-rights officer to each of its regional bureaus and appointed "an assistant legal adviser for human rights" to oversee the department's human-rights policies.

Human-rights advocates in Congress regarded the reorganization of the State Department as a major achievement of the human-rights campaign. But they also believed that the campaign had achieved other notable results. In 1977 Representative John Brademas (Democrat, Indiana), the majority whip of the House, listed three of these achievements. (1) Congress had established human-rights principles for American foreign policy. (2) It had overseen implementation of those principles. (3) It had voted to withdraw money for foreign assistance based on human-rights records.

In 1978 Robert Russell, the counsel for the Subcommittee of International Finance of the House of Representatives, declared that Congress had begun to work human-rights provisions "into every corner of U.S. law pertaining to international economic transactions."

But perhaps Representative Tom Harkin summed up the human-rights achievements of Congress best when he stated: "We have established a body of law that will be hard to reverse; precedents have been set for the State Department and others."

Precedents on human rights had indeed been established by Congress. These precedents would be taken up and expanded by President Jimmy Carter when he took office in 1977. Congress had taken the first step and had met with both successes and failures. Carter was to take the second step and attempt to make human rights, in his own words, "the cornerstone of our foreign policy."

CHAPTER

3

PRESIDENT
JIMMY CARTER
AND
HUMAN RIGHTS

I want to see our country set a standard of morality. I feel very deeply that when people are put in prison without trial and tortured and deprived of basic human rights that the President of the United States ought to have a right to express displeasure and do something about it. . . . I want our country to be the focal point for deep concern about human beings all over the world.

President Carter
at a town meeting in
Clinton, Massachusetts
March 1977

When Jimmy Carter became president in January 1977, he moved quickly to give human rights a central position in his foreign policy. During the presidential campaign of 1976 he had mentioned the importance of human rights on several occasions. A strong human-rights position, he had declared, would help to "make Americans feel proud again" about their nation's goals and ideals.

In his inaugural address, Carter made his position clear. "Our commitment to human rights," he said, "must be absolute, our laws fair, our national beauty preserved; the powerful must not persecute the weak, and human dignity must be enhanced."

"Because we are free," he went on, "we can never be indifferent to the fate of freedom elsewhere. Our moral sense dictates a clear preference for those societies which share with us an abiding respect for human rights."

Four months later, on May 22, 1977, Carter again reiterated his firm belief in human rights and linked human rights to American foreign policy. "Our belief," he said, is "that dignity and freedom are fundamental spiritual requirements."

"It is a new world," he continued, "that calls out for a new American foreign policy—a policy based on constant decency in its values and on optimism in our historic vision."

Carter's call for a new foreign policy created interest abroad. *The Times* of London said that it was a "stirring vision." The *London Financial Times* pointed out that "the world not only calls for a new American foreign policy, it is actually getting it."

Carter's concern for human rights derived from his Christian faith and his belief in the equality of all men and women under God. It also derived from his experiences in his native Georgia during the civil rights movement when he witnessed black Americans struggling to obtain rights and freedoms long denied them.

The new president's understanding of foreign policy had been deeply influenced by the thought and writings of Zbigniew Brzezinski, a Columbia University professor. Indeed, Carter was so impressed by Brzezinski that he appointed him to the post of national security adviser, one of the most powerful and significant positions in the new administration.

Brzezinski had developed his position on world affairs in a 1970 book entitled *Between Two Ages.* "The old framework of international politics," Brzezinski wrote, "is clearly no longer compatible with reality." The world, he believed, was ready to discard the traditional policies that had guided the relationships between nations for centuries.

Traditional foreign policy, Brzezinski explained, had been concerned with problems such as military alliances between nations and conflicts arising over differences of doctrine or ideology. Moreover, he went on, traditional foreign policy had developed in an age when the nations of Europe dominated world affairs. But that age is now over, Brzezinski claimed, and the kind of foreign policy characteristic of that age must also come to an end. Europe is no longer at the center of world affairs and the world is rapidly moving toward a point where every region is of equal importance.

The United States, Brzezinski declared, must develop new policies to meet this new state of affairs. Foreign policy, he wrote, must now be made to reflect an attitude of "rational humanism." It must also reflect a "global" perspective on world affairs, rather than a limited national or regional perspective.

In this new age of foreign policy, Brzezinski argued, international problems must be viewed as "human issues" and not as "political confrontations." The new American foreign policy, he concluded, must make "a broader effort to contain the global tendencies toward chaos," while helping the world to move toward a "community of developed nations."

Human rights was an important part of Brzezinski's vision of a new foreign policy. During the early days of the Carter administration, he advised the president to take a strong initiative on human rights. Previous administrations, he told the president, had ignored the problem of human rights and there had been a "striking decline in the relevance of the American message to the world." But by emphasizing human rights, he claimed, "America could again make itself the carrier of human hope" and "the wave of the future." Human rights could be the issue by which America won the hearts and minds of the people of the world.

Brzezinski also believed, however, that in pursuing human rights, the United States could never allow its power and strength to decline. For without "credible American power," he told the president, "we would simply not be able either to protect our interests or to advance more humane goals."

Cyrus Vance, Carter's secretary of state, also believed in the importance of human rights. At a news conference in late January 1977, he first stated his views on how the State Department would handle human-rights issues. "We will speak frankly about injustice both at home and abroad," Vance declared. "We do not intend, however," he continued, "to be strident or polemical, but we do believe that an abiding respect for human rights is a human value of fundamental importance and that it must be nourished."

"We will not comment on each and every issue," he concluded, "but we will from time to time comment when we see a threat to human rights, when we believe it is constructive to do so."

In a speech delivered at the Georgia Law School in Athens, Georgia, on April 30, 1977, Vance became specific about human rights. It was the first comprehensive statement on the issue by a member of the Carter administration. Vance put forth three sets of what he called "complementary and mutually reinforcing" rights. The first set included the "right to be free from governmental violation of the integrity of the person." Such violations, he said, included "torture; and arbitrary arrest or imprisonment." The first set, he added, also included the "denial of fair public trial and invasion of the home."

Vance's second set of human rights encompassed social and economic rights such as the "vital needs" of "food, shelter, health care, and education." The third set, he stated, were the "right to enjoy civil and political liberties" such as freedom of thought, religion, assembly, speech, and the press, as well as the freedom to take part in government and to move within and out of one's country at will.

Vance declared that the foreign policy of the Carter administration would be designed to deal with violations of each set of rights throughout the world. Nations that improved their records on human rights would win America's approval, while those that ignored the cause of human rights would gain its condemnation.

The Carter Administration in Action

The human-rights priorities of the Carter administration were listed in Presidential Directive 30, issued on February 17, 1978, but these priorities had already begun to emerge months earlier in State Department policy and practice. Among the most important points made by the directive were the following:

(1) That the *primary objectives* of the administration would be the worldwide reduction of governmental violations of the integrity of the person and the enhancement of civil and political liberties. The promotion of social and economic rights was deemed *important*, but not of primary importance.

(2) That the administration adopt "positive" measures on human rights. This meant that loans and assistance would be granted to nations improving their human-rights performance as a kind of reward.

(3) That the administration would grant no American support "other than in exceptional circumstances" for police or internal-security forces to nations with serious human-rights violations.

To implement these goals, the Carter administration undertook a reorganization of the executive branch that continued throughout the first two years of the administration. At the Department of State, Cyrus Vance expanded and upgraded the Bureau of Human Rights and Humanitarian Affairs.

The office was granted a relatively large staff, which divided its efforts into areas of human-rights concern such as arms sales, the Helsinki Final Act, refugee affairs, international loans, and individual country and regional affairs.

To emphasize the importance Carter placed on human rights, the Coordinator of Human Rights and Humanitarian Affairs was ordered to make reports directly to the secretary of state. The coordinator also had easy access to the president, who valued the agency's reports.

Zbigniew Brzezinski, the national security adviser, established what he called a "Global Issues Cluster" on his National Security Council staff. The cluster, among other things, was to advise him regularly on human-rights issues and how those issues might be worked into foreign policy.

To deal with the problem of financial aid and human rights, the Carter administration established the Inter-Agency Group on Human Rights and Foreign Assistance. Headed by Deputy Secretary of State Warren Christopher, the group was charged with granting (or withholding) loans and assistance to nations based on their human-rights records.

During the Carter years, the Christopher group opposed over sixty loans to fifteen different nations, including South Korea, Paraguay, and Guinea. On the other hand, the group supported aid to nations in cases where it judged that the aid would serve what it called "basic human needs."

Under Carter, the State Department sent U.S. observers to meet with Chilean political leaders who opposed the repressive military dictatorship that governed their country. The observers heard stories about the dictatorship's use of torture, imprisonment without trial, and murder to silence political dissidents in Chile.

The State Department also sent observers to the trials of political dissidents in the Soviet Union, South Africa, and Thailand to see if the dissidents were given fair trials and just sentences. Efforts were likewise made to secure the release of political prisoners in South Korea.*

Concerned that American arms and military equipment were being used against innocent citizens by repressive governments abroad, the Carter administration cut back military assistance to Indonesia, the Philippines, and several other countries. It also worked to bring down the sale of American arms and ammunition to all foreign countries.

Two of the most controversial human-rights decisions made by the Carter administration involved Nicaragua and Iran. Both nations had been longtime friends and allies of the United States and both had received large sums of American economic and military aid. But both nations were governed by dictators—General Anastasio Somoza-Debayle in Nicaragua and Shah Reza Pahlavi in Iran—who ran highly repressive governments with clear violations of human rights. In the mid- and late-1970s, both dictators were facing strong opposition from armed and militant dissident groups.

Arguing that the United States should no longer attempt to stem the tide of change in Nicaragua, the Carter administration withdrew its support of the Somoza regime, which rapidly fell

*The Carter human-rights policy toward South Korea, South Africa, and the Soviet Union will be discussed in greater detail in later chapters. These three countries have been singled out for separate chapters because each reveals, in striking detail and in very different ways, the difficulty of combining an effective human-rights policy with foreign affairs.

from power. It was replaced by a government run by the Sandinistas, a group of leftists with strong ties to Fidel Castro and the Cuban communist government.

The Carter administration was more supportive of the Shah of Iran but nevertheless demanded that he make significant improvements in Iran's human-rights record. Rightly or wrongly, the Shah believed that these demands undermined his control of the country, leaving him unable to deal with his political opponents. In 1979 the Shah was driven from power and replaced by a virulently anti-American government run by Islamic fundamentalists.

The Carter Human-Rights Policy:
Pros and Cons

One of the most notable triumphs of the Carter human-rights policy was the strong approval it received from human-rights experts and victims of repression abroad.

In the April 7, 1979, issue of *The New Republic*, for example, David Hawk, who was then an official with Amnesty International, wrote that "anyone who worked in the field of human rights before Carter became president can appreciate the difference he makes."

Support also came from South America. On April 30, 1978, Elio Gaspari, a Brazilian journalist, authored a guest editorial in *The New York Times*. The editorial carried the enthusiastic title "Carter Si!" Gaspari declared that "from the moment Latin Americans, Africans, and Asians started looking at President Carter as a politician interested in human rights, the United States Embassy ceased being seen by thousands as a headquarters for conservative maneuvers; it became identified with the nation it represents."

Support too came from China. In Peking in early 1979 a poster placed anonymously on a public wall called upon Carter to take notice of human-rights violations in China. Carter's interest in human rights in foreign lands was just and proper, the poster said, because when human-rights abuse occurs in one country it affects all mankind.

Carter administration officials welcomed the approval from abroad and felt encouraged by it. But they also believed that they had achieved more tangible results in the improvement of human rights abroad, especially in three areas: the treatment of political prisoners; the Panama Canal Treaty; and the establishment of "majority rule" in the African nation of Zimbabwe, formerly called Rhodesia.

Due to human-rights efforts by the Carter administration, the government of Peru released over three hundred political prisoners in April 1977. In Argentina the number of "disappearances" of political dissidents dropped from thousands per year in the mid-1970s to forty-four in 1979 and continued to drop.

By his personal intervention and appeal, President Carter was able to obtain the release of jailed Argentine journalist Jacobo Timerman. Timerman, who deeply opposed the military dictatorship that ruled his native country, left Argentina and later wrote a book exposing the dictatorship's human-rights violations.

In Chile General Pinochet, the head of the military junta, agreed to release political prisoners. Between 1977 and 1980, the government of Indonesia freed over thirty-five thousand political prisoners. Both Chile and Indonesia were responding to human-rights pressure from the Carter administration.

President Carter regarded the 1977 Panama Canal Treaty as a major achievement in human rights because it signaled a new and "more equitable relationship with South American nations and a new American attitude towards the rights of South American peoples." Previous administrations, Carter believed, had negotiated with attitudes of superiority and arrogance when dealing with South Americans. He hoped, however, that he had changed that state of affairs by dealing with them on a fair and equal basis. The provisions of the treaty allowed Panama to take control of the Canal by the end of the century.

One of the proudest achievements of the Carter administration was its African policy. When he came to the presidency, Carter had appointed Andrew Young, a black congressman, to be the American ambassador to the United Nations. Young had worked hard in his position—and was successful—in improving America's relationship with black African nations.

One of the thorniest African problems faced by the administration was the nation of Rhodesia. Rhodesia was ruled by a small white minority and its large black population had no rights at all. Black guerrilla bands were in open rebellion against the white regime and Rhodesia faced an uncertain future.

Carter officials, however, in concert with black and white leaders in Rhodesia, negotiated a successful transfer of power from the all-white government to a government in which all races could participate. By the end of the 1970s, white Rhodesia had emerged as the new multiracial government of Zimbabwe.

In his memoirs, *Power and Principle* (1983), Zbigniew Brzezinski summed up what he believed to be the overall human-rights achievements of the Carter administration. "It was Carter's accomplishment," Brzezinski wrote, "that, by the time he left office, there was more widespread appreciation worldwide that America stood again for principle and identified itself with the movement for more social and political justice.

"It is no exaggeration," he went on, "to say that, thanks to Carter, America was again seen, after the years of Watergate and Vietnam War, as standing for its traditional value of freedom. That is an asset in world affairs," he concluded, "that cynics are wrong to dismiss."

Nevertheless, the Carter human-rights policy did have its critics and its problems. A number of America's closest allies—including West Germany and the United Kingdom—were distinctly uncomfortable with Carter's emphasis on human rights and believed that it played against their own national interests. Chancellor Helmut Schmidt of West Germany, for example, regarded President Carter as dangerously naive in foreign policy and feared that the human-rights campaign would anger the Soviet Union and work against the delicate relationship that existed between the U.S.S.R. and the nations of Western Europe.

In America, too, there was widespread dissatisfaction with Carter's mixture of human rights and foreign policy. After the collapse of Iran and Nicaragua to strongly anti-American regimes, many Americans began to wonder if the Carter policy was costing America its friends and gaining nothing in return.

Indeed, by the end of his administration Carter himself had begun to doubt the propriety of a single-minded emphasis on human rights. Early in 1979 a coup d'etat in the tiny Caribbean nation of Grenada had overthrown a democratically elected government and replaced it with a dictatorship friendly to Cuba and the Soviet Union. Already smarting from the fall of Nicaragua to a leftist government, the Carter administration viewed with great displeasure what it regarded as a further advance of Soviet interests in the Western Hemisphere.

In November 1979 mobs of irate Iranians charged the United States embassy in Teheran and took 65 Americans hostage. For the next thirteen months, the last months of his administration, Carter exhausted much of his time and energy in an effort to negotiate the release of the prisoners.

Then in December 1979 the Soviet Union invaded Afghanistan, hoping to subdue that nation into obedience to a Soviet-sponsored Afghan government. President Carter denounced the Soviet invasion and attempted to rally support throughout the world for condemnation of the U.S.S.R.

Under pressure from events like those in Grenada, Iran, and Afghanistan, the idealistic foreign policy of the early Carter years began to fall apart. Carter continued to support human rights but now joined that support with a firm declaration of the need for America to be strong and powerful.

In a speech delivered in Philadelphia on May 9, 1980, for example, President Carter stated that foreign policy "must be based simultaneously on the primacy of certain basic moral principles—principles founded on the enhancement of human rights—and on the preservation of an American military strength that is second to none." Foreign policy, he went on, must be a "fusion of power and principle." This fusion, he concluded, "is the only way to ensure global stability and peace while we accommodate to the inevitable and necessary reality of global change and progress."

By the time he spoke in Philadelphia, however, Carter had become an unpopular president with an unpopular foreign policy. The Soviet invasion of Afghanistan had aroused fears of Soviet aggression and intentions in world affairs. Reports that Soviet military power had surpassed that of the United States caused worry about America's future. To many Americans human rights had become an issue of minor importance. Questions of U.S. power and strength now dominated political discussion in the country.

In the presidential election of November 1980, Carter was overwhelmingly defeated by Ronald Reagan, a conservative Republican. During the campaign Reagan had said little about human rights but had promised to restore America's military might and its power and influence abroad. Reagan referred to Carter as a "failed" president and declared that a Reagan administration would follow new policies and set new goals for American foreign policy. What those policies and goals were to be, we shall find out in the next chapter.

CHAPTER
4
THE REAGAN FOREIGN POLICY

We don't care whether we are liked by the rest of the world—we want to be respected.

Ronald Reagan during the
1980 presidential campaign

When he came to the presidency, Ronald Reagan believed that American foreign policy faced two major problems. The first was the need to restore respect for the United States throughout the world. The second was the Soviet Union.

Respect for America aboard, he believed, had declined during the 1970s, and it was now time to reverse that trend. If America were to play an influential and significant role in world affairs, it had to be regarded as strong and powerful, not as weak and indecisive.

But Reagan's chief concern was the growth and expansion of Soviet power and influence. During the previous decade, he said, Marxist governments had come to power in Nicaragua, Grenada, Angola, Ethiopia, Mozambique, and elsewhere. Each of these governments, he noted, was loyal to the Soviet Union and each was deeply anti-American. Moreover, he warned, the number of Marxist governments in the world was likely to continue to grow unless the United States opposed and withstood the spread of Soviet power and influence with firmness and determination.

Reagan was not an opponent of human rights. He deeply believed in the importance of civil and political liberties and in the American democratic tradition. But he also believed that President Carter had been wrong to mix human rights and foreign policy.

Carter's human-rights campaign, Reagan felt, had failed to achieve worthwhile ends. Moreover, he feared that Carter's deep concern for human rights had diverted his attention from far more important issues such as the decline of respect for America and the spread of Soviet power.

Reagan regarded Iran as one of the most striking examples of the failure of Carter's foreign policy. If America had acted to support the Shah completely and without hesitation, Reagan claimed during the presidential campaign of 1980, "there wouldn't have been a successful revolution" in Iran and the Shah, an American "ally of thirty-some-odd years standing," would have remained in power.

Instead of coming to the aid of the Shah in his time of need, Reagan charged, the Carter administration had demanded that he undertake reforms to improve human rights in Iran. As a result, the Shah's pro-American government collapsed and was replaced by a strongly anti-American government.

Carter's policy had failed to achieve its immediate goal of improving human rights in Iran, Reagan pointed out, because human-rights abuse was more widespread under the new government than it had been under the Shah. But more significantly, Reagan concluded, Carter's policy was a failure because it had cost the United States the loss of a loyal ally and had led to a precipitous decline in American influence in the Middle East.

In cases like Iran, Reagan believed that it was best to tolerate and ignore human-rights abuse. When nations are "proven friends" of the United States, he said, they should be supported and encouraged, rather than denounced and condemned. In a world where Soviet power was on the rise, he concluded, it was better to foster and preserve nations that were loyal to America than to lose their friendship and loyalty.

Iran was a "mistake" that Reagan wanted to avoid. He believed that it was America's responsibility to set an *example* as a land where freedom and human rights were cherished. But he thought it dangerous to the American national interest abroad to mix human rights with foreign policy as Jimmy Carter had done.

Jeane Kirkpatrick and Human Rights

Reagan's views on foreign policy were shaped by his conservative political principles. But they were also influenced by the thought and writings of Dr. Jeane Kirkpatrick, a former professor of political science at Georgetown University in Washington, D.C.

During the late 1970s Dr. Kirkpatrick emerged as one of the most articulate critics of the Carter human-rights campaign. In three widely read and widely discussed essays, she detailed her criticisms of Carter and outlined the direction she believed American foreign policy should take. In 1981 Kirkpatrick became the American ambassador to the United Nations, a cabinet-level position in the Reagan administration.

Dr. Kirkpatrick's first commentary on Carter policy was a short essay entitled "On the Invocation of Universal Values" and was published in 1978 in *Morality and Foreign Policy*, a collection of essays by a number of different authors. A longer, more comprehensive essay, "Dictatorships and Double Standards,"* appeared in the January 1979 issue of *Commentary* magazine. The third, "U.S. Security and Latin America," came out in the January 1981 issue of *Commentary*.

Dr. Kirkpatrick began by praising Carter's emphasis on human rights. The Carter campaign for human rights, she wrote, had helped to remind Americans "and the rest of the world that this nation's identity and purposes are deeply involved with the assertion of universal human rights." Moreover, she went on, Carter had given the American government a voice of high moral principle and a commitment to the notion "that there are universal moral rights that men as men (and women as women) are entitled to and that these rights ought to be respected by government."

These were significant achievements, Kirkpatrick admitted. Her disagreement with the Carter foreign policy, she explained, was not over the issue of human rights. It was over the way the president had put his policy into practice. Kirkpatrick believed that the Carter foreign policy had been too *passive* and too unwilling to assert American ideals and interests abroad. When social and political change came to nations like Iran and Nicaragua, she wrote, Carter and his advisers had tended to accept that change as inevitable and to believe that the best America could do about it was to learn to live with it.

The Carter people, she went on, saw world events as "manifestations of deep historical forces that cannot be controlled" by human effort or intervention. They likewise believed, she claimed, that all any government could do was "to serve as a 'midwife' to history, helping events to move where they are already headed." Kirkpatrick found this view of change and history profoundly mistaken and wrongheaded. It was wrong, she wrote, because any view of history that saw all change as inev-

---

*Reagan read this essay when it appeared and was deeply impressed by it. It led him to strike up a friendship with Dr. Kirkpatrick and later to appoint her ambassador to the United Nations.

itable and predetermined by "historical forces" left no room for individual response and decision making. Moreover, she added, it was wrong because it encouraged the belief that men and women are mere victims or pawns of history and can do nothing to alter or alleviate their fate.

Kirkpatrick believed that reasonable men and women had to reject this view of history and change. Individual decisions, she argued, do make a difference. Men and women are not the victims of history but can act to change the course of events and decide their own fate. Nations need not accept change, she wrote, when that change is bad and undesirable. If the Carter administration had pursued a more *active* foreign policy, Kirkpatrick claimed, it could have prevented Nicaragua and Iran from falling to highly repressive and anti-American regimes.

The case of Nicaragua particularly bothered her. Instead of coming to the support of the Somoza government, she noted, Carter had stood back, believing that change was inevitable in Nicaragua and that nothing could or should be done to prevent Somoza's fall. Carter assumed, Kirkpatrick wrote, that the armed conflict between the Nicaraguans who supported President Somoza and the Sandinista rebels "was the equivalent of a national referendum . . . that could be settled by the Nicaraguan people."

But this was simply not the case, she maintained. The Somoza regime was not defeated by popular will that was expressed in a free and open referendum or election. It was defeated by a rebel force that was receiving large supplies of arms and ammunition from outside Nicaragua—primarily from communist Cuba. The Sandinista rebels, she insisted, did not represent the views of the average Nicaraguan. They expressed only the power that comes from having a gun and being willing to use it. Had Carter acted to support Somoza, she believed, and not let events take their course, the Sandinistas would have been defeated and a repressive Marxist government would not be in control of Nicaragua today.

Dr. Kirkpatrick was not an admirer of President Somoza. She recognized that he had run a repressive government with a poor record on human rights. But she believed that the Somoza regime, with all its faults, was preferable to the left-wing government that had emerged under the leadership of the Sandinistas.

Carter had failed to realize that the Somoza government was preferable to the Sandinistas in Nicaragua, Kirkpatrick believed, because he was the victim of two dangerous prejudices and misconceptions. The first was a prejudice against right-wing, *au-*

thoritarian governments like that of Somoza when he was in power. The second was a prejudice in favor of left-wing revolution.

Carter and other like-minded advocates of human rights, Kirkpatrick noted, have a strong dislike for right-wing, authoritarian governments such as those that existed in prerevolutionary Iran and Nicaragua. They dislike the extremes of wealth and poverty characteristic of authoritarian societies and are sickened by the lack of concern the wealthy show for the poor. They are also troubled by the low standards of justice and efficiency in such nations and by repression and human-rights abuse.

But human-rights advocates are deeply mistaken, Kirkpatrick went on, if they conclude that left-wing revolution will lead to less injustice, greater freedom, and fewer instances of human-rights abuse. Left-wing revolutionaries, she warned, speak only the "rhetoric" of democracy and human freedom. When they come to power, they are far more repressive—and far less sensitive to human-rights issues—than are right-wing authoritarian governments.

Many right-wing authoritarian governments, Kirkpatrick noted, may have poor records on human rights, but at least they do follow traditional patterns of life that help make life bearable for their citizens. Authoritarian societies, she argued, "do not disturb the habitual rhythms of work and leisure, habitual places of residence, habitual patterns of family and personal relations." Such societies likewise, she continued, "worship traditional gods and observe traditional taboos" and "create no refugees."

But "precisely the opposite is true of revolutionary Communist regimes," Kirkpatrick wrote. "They create refugees by the millions because they claim jurisdiction over the whole life of society and make demands for change that so violate internalized values," she concluded, "that inhabitants flee in the remarkable expectation that their attitudes, values, habits, and goals will 'fit' better in a foreign country than in their native land."

Furthermore, Kirkpatrick went on, right-wing authoritarian governments have proved themselves capable of liberalization and democratization. Both Spain and Portugal were once governed by authoritarian dictatorships but have since changed to become democracies with good records on human rights.* To

---

*When it held free and democratic elections at the end of 1983, the Argentine republic joined Spain and Portugal on the list of formerly authoritarian governments that have transformed themelves into democracies.

date, however, Kirkpatrick insisted, there has been *no* instance of a left-wing totalitarian government moving in the direction of greater liberalization and democratization. Since right-wing governments have proved themselves capable of change and improvement, Kirkpatrick asked, are they not preferable to left-wing revolutionary governments?

In conclusion, Kirkpatrick asked her readers to note that right-wing regimes were "more compatible with U.S. interests" than are left-wing regimes. Right-wing governments, she claimed, were rarely vehemently anti-American, like most left-wing governments, and right-wing governments have more often proved themselves open to American suggestion.

Dr. Kirkpatrick's essays were a plea for greater realism in the pursuit of human rights. Right-wing dictatorships should be tolerated, she believed, because they can evolve into genuine democracies, because they are less repressive than left-wing regimes, and because they are more compatible with American interests. But above all, Kirkpatrick wanted her readers to realize that the chief threat to human rights and freedom today comes from left-wing, communist governments. Had President Carter been serious about his human-rights campaign, she claimed, he would have attempted the "destabilization" of a communist government, as he had caused the destabilization of Nicaragua and Iran. But he had not, and this, for her, was proof that the Carter human-rights campaign had lacked consistency and genuine dedication to the cause of human rights.

The Reagan Administration and Human Rights

The Reagan administration has developed no clear-cut and outspoken position on human rights and foreign policy. Nevertheless, it has undertaken several actions that involve human-rights issues and that give an indication of its attitude toward human rights. Some of these measures were negative and were concerned with nothing more than undoing the Carter heritage on human rights. Others were more positive and designed to establish a Reagan position on how America might foster human rights abroad.

Among the most significant steps undertaken by the Reagan administration are the following:

■ Soon after taking office in 1981, Reagan removed several senior State Department officials who had been influential in implementing Carter's policy toward Nicaragua. The officials were replaced by men and women who would be likely to take a hard line against further Marxist revolutions in the area.

- The Reagan administration at first postponed and then comletely suspended American aid to the Sandinista government in Nicaragua. Other administration actions were also directed against the Sandinistas. Anti-Sandinista Nicaraguans were allowed to train in Florida in preparation for an invasion of Nicaragua and there were rumors in the world press that the CIA. was clandestinely involved in efforts to destabilize and overthrow the Sandinista regime. In addition, American military aid was increased to Central American nations such as Honduras, which borders on Nicaragua but remains friendly to the United States. American support was also given to anti-Sandinista Nicaraguans who had formed guerrilla bands in Honduras and made sporadic raids into Nicaragua.

- On a number of occasions, President Reagan publicly denounced the Sandinista government for human-rights abuse. He accused the Sandinistas of destroying freedom of religion in Nicaragua and of brutal treatment of Nicaragua's Meskito Indians. He also attacked the Sandinista government for failing to hold free and open elections to test its popularity with the people.

- The Reagan administration lifted previous bans on Export-Import Bank loans to Chile and invited Chile to participate in joint naval exercises with the U.S. Navy. The Carter administration had excluded Chile from these activities on human-rights grounds. Reagan likewise began to eliminate restrictions on military aid to Argentina and Uruguay.

- In the area of economic development abroad, Reagan and his advisers emphasized the importance of increased reliance on private investment and the transfer of resources rather than outright loans or assistance from the American government. This was in keeping with the administration's often-repeated belief that it is better to rely on private funds for economic development than on government funds.

- Reagan strongly supported and encouraged the government of Prime Minister Edward Seaga of Jamaica. In 1982 Seaga, a moderate, won the prime ministership over leftist Michael Manley in a free and democratic election. Manley had been in office for ten years and was a close friend of Fidel Castro of Cuba. He had established close ties with communist Cuba and the U.S.S.R.

The Reagan administration looked upon Manley's defeat and Seaga's victory as a triumph for democracy and human rights and a defeat for the Soviet Union. President Reagan invited Seaga to Washington where he praised Seaga's policies and promised American aid and assistance to Jamaica.

■ The Reagan administration began efforts to stop and reverse the expansion of Soviet influence in Africa. It responded favorably to overtures to the nations of Western Europe and the United States by President Samora Machel of Mozambique.

During the 1970s Machel had declared himself a Marxist, turned to the Soviet Union for aid and assistance, and welcomed Soviet and Cuban advisers and military troops to Mozambique. In the 1980s, however, Mozambique faced enormous economic difficulties and a disastrous drought.

With no economic aid forthcoming from the U.S.S.R., Machel turned to the West for help. The Reagan administration believed that Western economic assistance and investment could be used to lure Machel out of the Soviet "orbit" and to develop closer ties with the United States and the West.

As of early 1984, negotiations with Mozambique were in preliminary stages. But the chances looked good for the steady removal of the Cuban troops and Soviet advisers and for the eventual liberalization of Mozambique's society.

■ But the most controversial foreign-policy decision that Reagan has made—and the one that stands in greatest contrast to the Carter foreign policy—was the decision to invade the tiny Caribbean island nation of Grenada.

In October 1983 the government of Maurice Bishop, the Marxist dictator of Grenada, was overthrown by a group of rebels who were further to the left than he had been. The rebels seized power and murdered Bishop and most of his closest advisers. They declared martial law in Grenada and warned that opponents of the new regime would be dealt with summarily.

Two weeks later President Reagan ordered American troops to occupy Grenada. His decision was made, he declared, at the request of the Conference of East Caribbean Nations, which feared that Grenada was becoming a base from which communist revolution would spread. Reagan also said that he had ordered the invasion to protect the lives of Americans who were students at a Grenadian medical school.

The invasion—which was accomplished quickly and with

little loss of life—was denounced in the United Nations as American interference into the private affairs of a foreign nation. The overwhelming majority of U.N. members voted to condemn the American action and to demand that American forces be removed from the island immediately. The invasion was similarly condemned by the Organization of American States.

Ambassador Jeane Kirkpatrick, however, strongly defended the invasion. A vicious, illegal government that had murdered former Prime Minister Bishop and his advisers, she pointed out to the U.N. General Assembly, had been eliminated. Democratic and free elections would soon be held in Grenada, Kirkpatrick promised, and the Grenadans themselves would be allowed to choose the leaders and government they wanted. The Grenadan invasion, she concluded, had been a major victory for the cause of human rights. A totalitarian communist regime had been erased and democracy in Grenada was now a possibility.

It was unlikely that the Reagan administration would follow up the invasion of Grenada with other similar invasions of leftist nations. Yet the Grenadan invasion had made the Reagan position dramatically clear. Where it was possible, the United States would work to eliminate such regimes and replace them with governments that shared American values and goals. Clearly, the Reagan administration regarded Marxist governments as the greatest threat to U.S. interests abroad and the chief threat to human freedom and dignity.

But there were problems with the Reagan policy. Obviously, American military power could not be used to eliminate every totalitarian government in the world or even a few of them. As strong as America was, it did not have that kind of resources, nor would the American people support such a campaign. Furthermore, the Reagan policy was one of confrontation. It pitted American interests and values against Soviet interests and values and was likely to increase the tensions and enmities between the world's two most powerful nations.

It should be noted that from the beginning, the Reagan foreign policy moved in the direction outlined by Dr. Jeane Kirkpatrick in her three essays. It was a vigorous and active foreign policy that defined communism as America's enemy and that firmly supported nations which were regarded as "proven friends." It was also a foreign policy willing to assert the American national interest abroad and willing to use America's power and strength to make American influence felt in foreign lands. It was a foreign policy unlikely to sit back and let world events take whatever course they might take. Whether it will prove to be a successful foreign policy, however, remains to be seen.

CHAPTER
5
HUMAN RIGHTS AND THE AMERICAN HERITAGE

There are those who will say that the liberation of humanity, the freedom of man and mind, is nothing but a dream. They are right. It is the American dream. . . . The cause of human liberty is now the great revolutionary cause.

Archibald MacLeish

We Americans are at our best when we are true to ourselves. . . . In fact, championing human rights is a national requirement for a nation with our heritage.

Cyrus Vance
Hard Choices:
Critical Years in America's
Foreign Policy (1983)

President Jimmy Carter often
claimed that his human-rights policy stood firmly in the American tradition of support for human freedom and dignity. "Because we are free," he said in his inaugural address, "we can
never be indifferent to the fate of freedom everywhere."

There can be no doubt, too, that President Reagan regarded
his foreign policy as firmly rooted in American tradition and
practice. Can both presidents have been right? The answer, as
we shall see in this chapter, is a definite and clear-cut yes.

Americans, from the Founding Fathers to the present day,
have always championed the cause of human rights, as Carter
claimed. The advance of freedom and liberty has been seen as a
special American mission and goal. But it is also true that the
United States never pursued an active human-rights policy
abroad until the twentieth century. Before that, Americans had
very different ideas about their nation's role in world affairs.

The Founding Fathers, for example, wanted America to
serve as a model that other nations might imitate or follow.
America's responsibility, they believed, was to cultivate and
develop its own free institutions and limited form of government
rather than attempt to export the ideals of the American Revolution to foreign lands. Albert Gallatin, a close friend of Thomas
Jefferson and secretary of the treasury in Jefferson's cabinet,
wrote in this vein when he told his fellow Americans that "your
mission was to be a model for all governments, and for all less
favored nations." You Americans, he went on, must "adhere to

the most elevated principles of political morality" and "apply all your faculties to the gradual improvement of your own institutions and social state; and by your example . . . exert a moral influence most beneficial to mankind at large."

Benjamin Franklin likewise believed that America's example might have a salutary effect on the behavior and performance of other nations. "Establishing the liberties of America," he declared, "will not only make the people happy, but will have some effect in diminishing the misery of those, who in other parts of the world groan under despotism, by rendering it more circumspect, and inducing it to govern with a light hand."

Neither Gallatin nor Franklin, however, believed that the United States should insist that other nations follow America's example, nor did they believe that America's rights and freedoms should be made a part of American foreign policy. They recognized that the young republic was too new and weak to have a significant influence in world affairs. Furthermore, they feared that close involvement with other nations might lead to the corruption of American values. America, they believed, should remain isolated as much as possible from the rest of the world.

This was also the belief of the other Founding Fathers. In the 1790s a great enthusiasm for the French Revolution spread throughout the United States. Many Americans looked upon the French Revolution as a re-enactment of the American Revolution and hoped that it would bring democracy and civil liberties to France. Pro-French Americans held large rallies in support of the French revolutionaries and demanded that the American government grant aid and assistance to the French.

President George Washington, however, refused to be moved by the demands. He publicly denounced what he called the "love-frenzy for France" and kept American foreign policy on a course of strict neutrality in European affairs. In his farewell address to the nation on September 17, 1796, Washington explained the reason for his refusal to espouse the cause of the French revolutionaries and to come to their aid and support. "The nation which indulges toward another an habitual hatred or an habitual fondness," Washington warned, "is in some degree a slave." It is a slave to "its animosity or to its affection," he explained, "either of which is sufficient to lead it astray from its duty and its interest." Washington urged his fellow countrymen to stand aloof from the problems of other nations except "for extraordinary emergencies." He believed it was best for Americans to tend to their own problems rather than become involved in entangling commitments and responsibilities abroad.

In the early 1800s there was widespread support in America for the peoples of Latin America who were struggling to overthrow their colonial master, Spain, and establish independent nations. Once again, the spirit of freedom and democracy seemed to be on the move and once again many Americans urged that their government come to the support of revolutionaries in the name of freedom and human rights. In 1818 in the House of Representatives, Henry Clay (Whig, Kentucky) delivered a speech that warmly praised the Latin Americans. "We behold," Clay said, "the glorious spectacle of eighteen millions of people, struggling to burst their chains and to be free." Clay's speech was translated into Spanish and enthusiastically received by revolutionaries throughout Latin America.

In the early 1820s a "Greek fever" overtook Americans when they received news of the Greek struggle for independence against the Ottoman Empire. In 1823 President Monroe publicly offered his hopes for Greek success and for the establishment of freedom and liberty in Greece, the nation where democracy had been born.

The U.S. government, however, offered no aid or support to the Latin American revolutionaries, in spite of public clamor in favor of such support. Nor was any government support forthcoming for the Greek freedom fighters. John Quincy Adams, the secretary of state in Monroe's cabinet, explained why. "Wherever the standard of freedom and independence has been or shall be unfurled," he declared, "there will be America's heart." But the United States, he went on, "does not go abroad in search of monsters to destroy. She is the well-wisher to the freedom and independence of all." But, he concluded, "she is the champion and vindicator only of her own."

Once the nations of Latin America had won their independence from Spain, however, the U.S. government did act to guarantee that independence. On December 2, 1823, President Monroe announced the Monroe Doctrine, which declared the Western Hemisphere off limits to the nations of Europe. The Monroe Doctrine was the first major foreign-policy statement by the United States with important international ramifications. It combined a concern for the freedom and independence of the new Latin American nations with an even greater concern for America's own national interests.

President Monroe declared that "the American continents, by the free and independent condition which they have assumed and maintain, are henceforth not to be considered as subjects for future colonization by any European powers." Because "the political system" of European nations "is essentially different . . . from that of America," the president explained, "we should consider any attempt on their part to extend their system to any portion of this hemisphere as dangerous to our peace and safety."

The Monroe Doctrine did not apply to the European colonies that still existed in South and Central America. "With the existing colonies," President Monroe said, "we have not interfered and shall not interfere." But, he went on, "we could not view any interposition for the purpose of oppressing" the Latin American nations "or controlling in any other manner their destiny . . . in any other light than as the manifestation of an unfriendly disposition towards the United States."

In conclusion, the president stated that it was America's intention never to intervene in the affairs of Europe. "In the wars of European powers in matters relating to themselves," he pointed out, "we have never taken any part, nor does it comport with our policy so to do."

The Monroe Doctrine was a significant and bold step away from the vision of America as a model which other nations might imitate and follow. It was an expression of moral support and encouragement for the nations of Latin America. And, by implication, it committed American military power to the defense of the independent countries of the Western Hemisphere.

It is important to note, however, that the Monroe Doctrine had nothing to say about human rights. It did not urge the development of democratic institutions and made no connection between the state of civil liberties in Latin American nations and American support for their freedom and independence. Indeed, John Quincy Adams, who was largely responsible for the wording of the doctrine, had little hope that democracy could be established in Central and South America. There was, he declared at a cabinet meeting, "no prospect that they would establish free or liberal institutions of government. Arbitrary power," he explained, "military and ecclesiastical, was stamped upon their hearts, and upon all their institutions."

What the United States did promise in the Monroe Doctrine, however, was that the Latin American nations would be allowed to pursue their own policies, in their own way, without European interference. The doctrine also extended the principle of noninterference to the relationship between the United States and the nations of Europe. Just as America would not interfere in the internal matters of European countries, it declared, so European interference in American domestic concerns would not be welcome.

Throughout the nineteenth century the American government firmly adhered to this principle in its relationship with European governments. It was invoked on a number of occasions, but one stands out because it clearly revealed America's attitude at the time toward combining a concern for human rights with foreign policy.

During the late 1880s and the early 1890s, a series of anti-Italian riots occurred in many places in the United States. The riots were directed against Italian immigrants and frequently resulted in property damage, physical harm, and even death. In 1891, in New Orleans, a vigilante mob murdered eleven Italian-Americans. By any standards, the human rights of Italian immigrants in the United States had been violated. But when an outraged Italian government lodged an official protest with the American government over the treatment of Italian-Americans, James G. Blaine, the secretary of state, declared, "I do not recognize the right of any government to tell the United States what it should do."

Clearly, American foreign policy in the nineteenth century had no concept of "human rights," as those words were understood by the Carter administration. Americans of that time passionately regarded their country as an example for other nations to follow, but government policy did not go abroad to seek the establishment of democratic institutions and American values.

Human Rights and American Foreign Policy in the Twentieth Century

In part, the reluctance of the U.S. government to commit itself abroad to the advance of democracy and freedom had been due to America's relative weakness and insignificance in world affairs. It would have been unreasonable to assume that a young, developing nation could have brought its influence to bear on older, more established, and more powerful nations.

By the end of the nineteenth century, however, America had itself developed into one of the powerful nations of the earth. With a population of seventy-six million, it was one of the most populous of countries. But it was also wealthy and prosperous and was blessed with abundant natural resources and with rapidly growing and enormously productive industries.

The growth of American power and strength gave America a new position in international relations and led to significant changes in American foreign policy. The nation that had once been reluctant to become involved abroad now sought to win a place in world affairs that equaled its enormous power and strength.

But the role America has played as a world power has been inconsistent. At times, the United States has pursued a vigorous foreign policy that included an emphasis on human-rights issues. At other times, it has withdrawn from commitments and involvement abroad and preferred to tend to its own problems.

Consider the following examples:

▪ As a result of the Spanish-American War of 1898, the United States acquired the Philippines. The acquisition of a colony presented the nation with a moral dilemma. Many Americans believed that America, which had once been a colony itself, should never have colonies of its own.

Other Americans wanted the United States to take possession of the Philippines as a sign of America's new power and strength in world affairs. President William McKinley was torn between the two positions. He saw that it might be wrong for the United States, the advocate of freedom and independence, to take charge of another nation.

But he also recognized that the Philippines were a valuable asset to American interests in the Far East. He resolved the issue by declaring the Philippines an American colony. But at the same time, McKinley stated that America's "mission" in the Philippines would be to help the Philippine people develop democratic institutions, establish civil liberties, and improve their lives.

▪ In 1903 President Theodore Roosevelt publicly condemned the persecution of Jews in czarist Russia. The Russian government responded by declaring that Roosevelt's statement was an invasion of Russia's private and domestic affairs. Nine years later, in 1912, President William Howard Taft withdrew an 1832 commercial agreement between the United States and Russia. The agreement, he said, could not remain in existence as long as Russia continued to mistreat its own Jewish people and American Jews of Russian descent who returned to their native land.

▪ The first president to pursue a vigorous human-rights policy abroad was Woodrow Wilson. In a 1914 speech, Wilson declared that he looked forward to the time when "America will come into the full light of day when all shall know that she puts human rights above all other rights and that her flag is the flag not only of America, but of humanity."

When the United States entered World War I in 1917, Wilson said that it was a war to make the world "safe for democracy." He went on:

This is a Peoples' War, a war for freedom and justice and self-government amongst all the nations of the world, a war to make the world safe for the peoples who live upon it. . . .

At the end of the war, Wilson was instrumental in the establishment of the League of Nations, an international organization that he hoped would foster peace, cooperation, and good will among nations. Wilson's last years in office were spent in an exhaustive effort to persuade the United States to join the League.

▪ Wilson's effort, however, was in vain. The U.S. Senate refused to approve America's membership in the League of Nations, and the mood of the nation was against extensive foreign entanglements. Many who opposed America's membership in the League did so out of a fear that membership in an international organization that included many repressive and dictatorial nations might corrupt American democracy. "You cannot yoke a government whose fundamental maxim is that of liberty," said Senator William Borah (Republican, Idaho), a leading opponent of League membership, "to a government whose first law is force and hope to preserve the former." "We may become one of the . . . dictators of the world," if America joins the League of Nations, he concluded, "but we shall no longer be master of our own spirit."

▪ During the administration of President Franklin Roosevelt, the United States once again began to develop an activist foreign policy with an emphasis on human rights. It was Roosevelt's vision that human rights would one day be recognized throughout the world.

On January 6, 1941, Roosevelt delivered his annual address to Congress. His speech was concerned with human rights and has come to be known as the "four freedoms speech." Roosevelt spoke at a time when the armies of Nazi Germany had overrun much of Europe, when a fascist government was in power in Italy, and when Japan had taken control of much of the Far East.

In his speech Roosevelt said that he looked forward "to a world founded upon four essential human freedoms." These freedoms, he went on, were first the "freedom of speech and expression—everywhere in the world."

"The second is freedom of every person to worship God in his own way—everywhere in the world."

"The third," Roosevelt declared, "is freedom from want—which, translated into world terms, means economic understandings which will secure to every nation a healthy peaceful life for its inhabitants—everywhere in the world."

"The fourth," Roosevelt concluded, "is freedom from fear—which, translated into world terms, means a worldwide reduction of armaments to such a point and in such a thorough fashion that no nation will be in a position to commit an act of physical aggression against any neighbor—anywhere in the world."

Roosevelt's speech was the most complete statement on human rights made by an American president up to his time. Eleven months after he spoke, however, the United States entered World War II, and Roosevelt's remaining years in office were spent in winning the war. He did not live to see his vision carried out.

■ Roosevelt's successor, President Harry Truman, was also a firm advocate of human rights. America is dedicated, Truman noted in a 1946 speech, "to the achievement and observation of human rights and fundamental freedoms. . . . Unless we can obtain these objectives for all men and women everywhere—without regard to race, language, or religion—we cannot have permanent peace and security."

Under Truman the United States joined the United Nations and committed itself to the United Nations Universal Declaration of Human Rights. Under Truman, too, America devoted large sums of time, money, and effort to the preservation of democracy in Western Europe and Greece and helped to establish a democratic government in Japan.

■ Not every American, however, shared Truman's enthusiasm for human rights. During his administration, opposition to American commitment to international agreements on human rights had begun to grow. The Senate refused to accept the U.N. Covenant on Civil and Political Rights, which established a Human Rights Committee to review human-rights violations throughout the world. It likewise refused to endorse the U.N.

Convention on the Prevention and Punishment of the Crime of Genocide and the U.N. Covenant on Economic, Social, and Cultural Rights.

In the early 1950s, Senator John Bricker (Republican, Ohio) proposed an amendment to the Constitution that would prevent America from agreeing to any treaty or declaration under which "any foreign power or any international organization" could "supervise, control, or adjudicate the rights of citizens of the United States within the United States."

The Bricker amendment was directed at America's membership in the United Nations and at its commitment to the Declaration of Human Rights. Bricker disagreed with the inclusion of economic and social rights among the rights advocated by the United Nations and the Declaration. "Social and economic rights," he declared, were "not rights or freedoms in any true sense." "They are not constitutional rights," he said, as Americans understand them, because the American constitution "was designed in the belief that mankind's aspirations can best be achieved through individual initiative." If the U.S. Senate approved the United Nations' list of social and economic rights, he warned, it would be the same as accepting "socialism by treaty." Bricker wanted the United States out of the United Nations and wanted its commitment to the Declaration of Human Rights annulled.

The Bricker amendment almost passed the Senate. When it came up for vote, sixty out of ninety-six senators voted in favor, only four short of the two-thirds necessary for ratification.

The Bricker amendment failed to pass, but its spirit lives. The Senate has never accepted the U.N. treaties on genocide, on social, economic, and cultural rights or the Covenant on Civil and Political Rights, even though many presidents have urged their passage.

▪ Since the end of World War II, the primary concern of U.S. foreign policy has been the American relationship with the Soviet Union and the communist world. Two wars have been fought against the communists: a successful one in Korea and an unsuccessful one in Vietnam.

But even the years between the wars have been tense and full of stress. Both superpowers, the United States and the U.S.S.R., have large stockpiles of nuclear weapons aimed at one another and capable of destroying the whole world many times over. Both nations seem incapable of resolving their differences and establishing a peaceful world order.

Human-rights issues have played a significant part in America's ongoing "cold war" with the Soviet Union. America has styled itself the defender of the free world against communist totalitarianism. Every American president since World War II has declared that America's responsibility in world affairs is to work for the preservation of democratic institutions in a world where those institutions are under threat of destruction.

In 1961, in his inaugural address, President John Kennedy stated America's cold war position on human rights and foreign policy with firmness and eloquence. "Let every nation know . . . ," Kennedy declared, "that we shall pay any price, bear any burden, meet any hardship, support any friend, oppose any foe, in order to assure the survival and the success of liberty." He also said that America was "unwilling to witness or permit the slow undoing of those human rights to which this nation has always been committed, and to which we are committed today at home and around the world."

Kennedy pledged that America would help to wipe out world poverty. And he pledged American support for the developing nations of the third world and spoke of a special relationship that should develop between the United States and the nations of Latin America.

Every American president for the past forty years could agree with Kennedy's words. Some might disagree with his sweeping proposals for aid and assistance abroad and argue that America's primary duty was to remain strong and united in its long struggle with the Soviet Union. But all would agree that if America stood for anything, it stood for human freedom and dignity and that the American position on human rights should be clear for the whole world to see. Where they disagreed was on how that position should be made clear.

In this chapter we have looked at the American heritage of human rights. That heritage, we must conclude, is broad enough to encompass both the administration of Jimmy Carter and that of Ronald Reagan. When Carter declared human rights to be the "soul" of American foreign policy, he was acting in the tradition of Woodrow Wilson and Franklin Roosevelt. Like those two presidents, he hoped that America's power and influence could be used to promote free institutions and better lives for people throughout the world. When Reagan declared that he didn't care whether the rest of the world liked America but wanted worldwide "respect" for the United States, he was acting in the tradition of those who believe that the best way to preserve free and democratic institutions is through strength and military preparedness.

The Carter approach has been called "idealistic" and "naive," the Reagan policy "realistic" and "cold-blooded." But both have enjoyed the support of women and men of good will, and both are likely to be the patterns followed by later presidential administrations in the search for a viable and workable combination of human rights and foreign policy.

CHAPTER

6

AN AFRICAN DILEMMA: THE CASE OF SOUTH AFRICA

Organized denial of human rights to all but seven-teen percent of its people on the grounds of their race make South Africa's "internal affairs" a matter of world concern.

Julius Nyerere
president of Tanzania
in *Foreign Affairs,*
July 1977

To an outsider, the changes that have taken place . . . may seem pitifully inconsequential, but anyone who remembers the South Africa of even five years ago will be startled to see black children swinging on swings in the public parks, or an Indian family eating a meal unhindered in an open-air restaurant.

South African novelist
Dan Jacobson
in *Commentary,*
March 1978

S outh Africa is a nation of thirty million people. Out of that thirty million, there are five million whites who enjoy every right and freedom that South Africa has to offer. The remaining twenty-five million people have few rights or none at all.

The five million whites can vote and hold public office. They can travel where they please, hold the most desirable and best-paying jobs, and rise to the highest levels of government and professional careers. The other twenty-five million cannot because racial separation—called *apartheid* or "apartness"—is the law in South Africa.

The world has condemned apartheid on many occasions. U.S. presidents have called upon the South African government to alter its racist policies. America has joined the overwhelming majority of nations in the United Nations in denouncing South Africa. But apartheid continues to exist. Why don't American leaders put more pressure on South Africa to reform? Why does the United States have any kind of relationship at all with a nation that denies basic human rights to more than 80 percent of its population?

The answer is simple: South Africa's enormous mineral wealth. South African mines produce roughly half the world's tonnage of gold each year and most of its diamonds. In addition, South Africa has about 81 percent of the world's known reserves of chrome, 75 percent of the manganese, 71 percent of the platinum, and 49 percent of the vanadium. It also has large deposits of antimony and andalusites.

South African gold helps to shore up the world's economy. Its other minerals are absolutely essential to modern industry. They are used in the production of high-quality steel and sophisticated alloys. They are also of fundamental importance to the chemical, petroleum, and electronic industries. The United States, therefore, tolerates apartheid because it must. Without a steady flow of South African mineral wealth to America, vital industries—many of which are connected with national defense—would have to shut down.

But the United States has paid a price for its toleration of apartheid. Many black African nations maintain cool relations with the United States because they believe that Washington could do more to bring down apartheid. If America exerted the influence it is capable of, they believe, apartheid would quickly collapse. Moreover, the Soviet Union has taken advantage of America's relationship with South Africa to spread anti-American propaganda throughout black Africa.

In this chapter, we shall look at the evils of apartheid and at the steps taken by the Carter and Reagan administrations in their dealings with the South African government.

Apartheid in Practice

South Africa is the only nation in the world today that practices racial discrimination by law, and its laws involve all aspects of society. A Population Registration Act, for example, assigns all persons to racial categories. These categories include three million "coloreds" (people of mixed descent), one million Asians (mostly people descended from Indians who immigrated to South Africa from India), and 21 million blacks.

A Group Areas Act requires that blacks, coloreds, and Asians reside in areas segregated from white residential areas. Black, colored, and Asian commercial establishments must also be segregated from white areas.

A 1952 law declared that blacks who lived in urban areas could not own homes, even though blacks had owned homes in urban areas up to that time. Permanent residence in urban areas was limited to those blacks who could prove that they had been born in the city, had lived there continuously for fifteen years, or had worked for the same employer for at least ten years.

In the same year, the Natives Act required all South African blacks to carry "reference books" listing their birthplace, their employment record, tax payments, and police record.

A 1953 law gave the government power to move black residents from their homes in Johannesburg to a new location twelve miles away. Since 1953 subsequent laws have permitted the forced removal of other blacks, Asians, and coloreds from their homes to new locations. Altogether, it is estimated that five hundred thousand nonwhites have experienced forced removal by government fiat.

A 1957 bill gave the government the power to decide who could visit a library or a place of entertainment. A 1959 bill made it difficult for nonwhites to attend South African universities, although nonwhites had been attending these universities for decades.

The South African government exercises censorship on all forms of media. A number of laws restricts what reporters can write on issues the government regards as controversial. A Publications Control Board censors all books, films, magazines, and even handbills.

The South African government has passed severe laws to deal with political dissent. South African police, for example, can jail prisoners without trial for as long as they want and without benefit of counsel or access to friends and relatives.

A special provision of the Internal Security Act allows the government to "ban" individuals it regards as subversive. When a person is "banned," he or she can live at home but can never talk or be with more than one other person at a time and must report regularly to the police.

South African police arrest between seven hundred and eight hundred blacks each year and jail them for failure to carry the required "registration form" with them at all times. Since the introduction of banning, well over one thousand people of all racial categories—including white—have been banned for their opposition to government policies.

South African police act quickly—and often harshly—to put down all antiapartheid protest. In 1960 between three thousand and twenty thousand blacks (estimates vary widely) presented themselves at the police station in the town of Sharpeville. None was carrying the "registration form." The police panicked and fired on the crowd, killing 68 and wounding 86. In protest of the "Sharpeville massacre," blacks in Capetown, Johannesburg, and elsewhere demonstrated and held work stoppages. In response the government arrested and jailed more than twelve thousand protesters. For the next several years, the police conducted a campaign designed to root out all black opposition and to arrest major black political leaders.

On June 16, 1976, a second tragedy occurred, similar to the Sharpeville massacre, when police opened fire on a crowd of ten thousand schoolchildren in Soweto. The schoolchildren were marching in protest of a recent government directive ordering elementary schools to teach half their subjects in Afrikaans,* rather than in English. During the weeks that followed, blacks rioted and demonstrated throughout South Africa. Government repression of the rioting was severe. During the first eleven months following the Soweto protest, at least 661 blacks were killed by the police and more than 4,000 were wounded. Most of the dead and wounded were young black males.

In the same period, more than one thousand blacks were arrested and eight hundred more were detained without trial. Police brutality and torture resulted in the deaths of a number of black leaders, including the widely admired Stephen Biko, the first president of SASO, the South African Students' Organization. Biko died in police custody in 1977, probably from beatings he had received. Just before he died, he had been shackled naked in his cell, then driven, still shackled and naked, over 750 miles in the back of a Landrover to a prison hospital. A coroner's report stated that he had had five brain lesions.

In response to the riots that followed the violence in Soweto, the government also closed down black organizations such as the Black Women's Federation and the Union of Black Journalists, as well as a number of other groups. It likewise banned leading opponents of apartheid, including Donald Woods, the white editor of the East London (South Africa) *Daily Dispatch,* who had been a friend and associate of Stephen Biko.

Under apartheid, blacks have no rights at all, while coloreds and Asians have a few privileges, but not many. Apartheid degrades the human dignity of the nonwhites of South Africa and allows them no means to protest their condition. By any standards, apartheid is a clear violation of basic human rights.

The United States and Human Rights in South Africa

The first American statement opposing apartheid came in 1958 when the United States voted along with the majority of nations

*Most South African whites are descended from English or Dutch ancestors. *Afrikaans* is the name for the kind of Dutch now spoken in South Africa, which differs slightly from the Dutch of Holland. Afrikaans-speaking South Africans called themselves Afrikanders, and it was they and not English-speaking South Africans who were largely responsible for the establishment of apartheid, which is an Afrikaans word. English is regarded as an acceptable language by South African blacks, while Afrikaans is often referred to as "the language of the oppressor." The schoolchildren at Soweto were marching in protest of the requirement that made them use the hated language.

in the U.N. General Assembly to condemn South Africa's racist policies.

Two years later, in 1960, the United States again voted with a majority in the United Nations to blame the South African government for the Sharpeville massacre.

In 1963, during the Kennedy administration, the United States declared an embargo on the shipment of American arms to South Africa. The embargo was undertaken to assure that American weapons would not be used against blacks in South Africa. It was also undertaken months before a U.N. vote that called for a similar embargo on arms shipments to South Africa by all U.N. members. In 1964 the Export-Import Bank suspended all direct loans designed to finance American exports to South Africa.

In 1973 the State Department issued guidelines for labor practices by American-owned corporations and industries in South Africa. These guidelines were designed to help reduce apartheid in the workplace and were voluntary—the firms involved were not required to follow them.

When the Carter administration came to power in January 1977, it began to stiffen the American opposition to apartheid. In May of that year, Carter's vice president, Walter Mondale, met in Vienna with South African president B. J. Vorster. Mondale told Vorster that the United States supported an end to racial discrimination and the guarantee of full participation of all citizens, of all races, in the South African government. Mondale pointed out that America did not demand that South Africa follow any given blueprint or timetable of reform, but he suggested that serious dialogue between white and black leaders in South Africa would be a significant first step.

The Mondale-Vorster meeting was one of several efforts undertaken by the Carter administration to improve America's relationship with black Africa and to underline U.S. opposition to apartheid. Others followed:

■   In 1977 the Carter administration banned the import of chrome from Rhodesia, a nation that, at that time, had a white-controlled government similar to South Africa's.

■   In August 1977 President Carter sent Andrew Young, the U.N. ambassador and black former congressman, as his personal representative to the Anti-Apartheid Conference in Lagos, Nigeria. The choice of Young, a personal friend of the president, was made to emphasize the administration's strong stand against apartheid.

- Also in 1977, the Carter administration extended the American ban on American arms shipments to South Africa to include other exports, such as any commercial equipment or spare parts intended for use by the South African police or military. The embargo was undertaken in reaction to the Soweto massacre and to the death of Stephen Biko.

  In South Africa the embargo provoked Prime Minister Vorster to denounce the United States as a greater threat to South Africa than "international communism." The prime minister accused the Carter administration of attempting to destroy his government by "strangulation with finesse" and vowed to resist all American efforts to pressure South Africa to dismantle apartheid.

- In April 1978, President Carter made a state visit to the African nations of Nigeria and Liberia. The president emphasized his interest in and concern for African affairs and was well received. The success of Carter's visit contrasted vividly with Secretary of State Kissinger's visit to Africa in 1976, when Kissinger's plane was refused permission to land in Lagos, Nigeria.

- In 1978 and 1979 Carter administration officials worked with black and white leaders in Rhodesia (now Zimbabwe) to produce a plan for majority rule in that country. In 1980, after free and democratic elections in which all races participated, a new government took power.

- During the Carter years, efforts were also made by private individuals and organizations to erase apartheid. The most significant of these efforts was the "Sullivan code," created by the Reverend Leon Sullivan, a black American civil rights activist and a member of the board of directors of General Motors.

  The Sullivan code was a list of six principles to be followed by American firms with plants and operations in South Africa. The principles were aimed at desegregation of facilities, equal pay for equal work, training and advancement for blacks, and the recognition of the right of South African blacks and other nonwhites to be union members and engage in collective bargaining. In 1980 Sullivan announced that 140 American firms with South African connections had agreed to the provisions of the code. Since that time, the Sullivan code has been adopted by a number of other foreign-owned businesses in South Africa and, in a few instances, by South African firms themselves.

  When the Reagan administration took office in January

1981, it immediately began to abandon the Carter policy toward South Africa. Reagan appointees in the State Department charged that the Carter policy had amounted to little more than heated rhetoric, rhetoric that angered South African leaders without producing results.

The Reagan administration opposed apartheid but believed that the best American policy toward South Africa was one of "constructive engagement." Constructive engagement meant that America would abandon its public pressure on South Africa to reform apartheid and would pursue all discussions on the subject through quiet diplomacy.

What are the chances for genuine change in South Africa? Most observers believe that they are slim, at least for the near future.

In November, 1983, in an all-white referendum, South Africans voted to accept new laws which established a three-house legislature. One house would be made up of white legislators; the second would be for coloreds and the third for Indians.

The new laws were carefully worded, however, to preserve white superiority in South Africa and South African blacks were not granted any representation in the new government at all.

There can be no doubt, however, that more change must someday come to South Africa. Observers note that black dissent and dissatisfaction is growing, in spite of government repression. The blacks of South Africa, the coloreds, and the Asians cannot be excluded from their civil and political rights forever.

Senator Nancy Kassebaum (Republican, Kansas), the chairman of the Senate Foreign Relations Subcommittee on Africa, visited South Africa in late 1982. Her views on the South African dilemma appeared in the *Washington Post* on February 15, 1983, in a column entitled "South Africa: It's Time We Acted."

"The daily indignities of black life inherent in apartheid," Kassebaum wrote, "—the restrictions on movement, the 'banning' of public figures, the separation of families—are repugnant to Americans and call for unequivocal U.S. opposition." The Reagan policy of "constructive engagement" with South Africa, she continued, was the correct attitude for America to take, because it was an attitude that did not alienate South African whites and kept the door open for dialogue.

But more needed to be done, Kassebaum claimed. Many black South Africans, she pointed out, believe that the Reagan administration does not care about their plight and look upon its policies as "a *carte blanche*" for South Africa "to pursue racial separation." Americans must come to recognize, she explained, that "quiet diplomacy alone has not achieved sufficient results in South Africa and needs to be supplemented with a stronger and more public stance."

Kassebaum suggested two steps that the United States might take to make its position on apartheid clear. First, it must press South Africa to pass a "bill of rights" that extends civil and political rights to all citizens, regardless of race or color. This bill of rights, she insisted, "should be a major U.S. policy goal."

Second, she suggested that the "State Department's human rights funds could be expanded to aid . . . selected social projects that address the needs of South African blacks." These two steps, she concluded, would clear up the mistaken notion that the Reagan administration is indifferent to apartheid and would help to improve America's image in Africa.

Kassebaum did not mention what kinds of pressure the United States might bring to bear upon South Africa. In the past all international efforts to bring down apartheid have been largely ignored by the South African government, and observers believe that South Africa is rich and powerful enough to resist stronger measures, such as a major economic boycott (which, in any case, would be undesirable because it would fall far more heavily on the shoulders of South African blacks and nonwhites than on the white population).

But South African observers believe, too, that time is running out. If a peaceful transition from apartheid to a multiracial society is to be carried out, it must be carried out soon, before South Africa is engulfed in a bitter and bloody racial war.

CHAPTER
7
HUMAN RIGHTS AND AMERICAN ALLIES: THE CASE OF SOUTH KOREA

How would you feel if a foreigner walked into the White House and told the President how to run his Government?

Philippine president
Ferdinand Marcos
quoted in *The New York Times*
April 16, 1978

We're still free and still Korean because of American sacrifices. Your people came here and died for a principle.

A South Korean
government official
quoted in *The Atlantic*
December 1983

O ne of the difficult problems faced by a human-rights policy is dealing with America's allies and friends. No nation, friend or foe, likes to be told what to do by another nation, but it is especially important to be cautious and circumspect when dealing with friends and allies.

South Korea is a loyal and longtime American ally. The United States helped to establish the Republic of Korea in 1948 and has devoted large amounts of aid and assistance to that country since that time. The two nations share an aversion to communism and a devotion to free enterprise and the capitalist system. Moreover, South Korea is regarded as essential to American interests in the Far East. American military bases in South Korea help provide protection from invasion by communist North Korea. They are also vital to the defense of Japan. For these reasons, it is important that South Korea remains friendly with the United States.

But South Korea also has a long record of human-rights abuse and repression. The dilemma faced by American policy-makers is a ticklish one: How can the South Korean government be persuaded to improve its human-rights record without embarrassing or angering this important American ally?

A Short History of South Korea

When the South Korean government was established in 1948, it adopted a democratic constitution based on the American Constitution. Its first president, Syngman Rhee, had studied at

Princeton University under Woodrow Wilson and professed admiration for American institutions.*

But Rhee did not govern in the American manner. Under him, all real political power in South Korea was concentrated in the president. The National Legislature was expected to do no more than give its stamp of approval to presidential policies and decision making. Rhee also began the practice of using hired thugs to harass and intimidate political opponents and dissidents. He likewise, on numerous occasions, ordered South Korean police to break up meetings and demonstrations by South Korean groups that opposed his policies. Every South Korean president since Rhee has continued these practices.

Between 1950 and 1953 the United States came to the aid of South Korea when South Korea was invaded by the army of communist North Korea. More than thirty-three thousand American soldiers died in that war, defending the independence of the South Koreans.

Following the end of the war, the United States made millions of dollars available to rebuild the shattered South Korean economy. American policymakers wanted South Korea to become a "showplace of democracy"—a nation where democracy and freedom flourished and that contrasted vividly with the repressive communist regime of North Korea.

American aid coupled with South Korean resourcefulness and hard work did produce what has been called an "economic miracle." South Korea became prosperous and productive. Its industries and businesses have been among the most successful in the world. But democracy did not fare so well. Throughout the four decades of its existence, South Korea has been governed by strongman presidents who have little regard for democratic institutions. The hope that South Korea might become a "showplace of democracy" never materialized.

The South Korean government has admitted that it does, on occasion, use repressive measures. But it has always defended these measures as necessary—given the circumstances under which South Korea exists. The South Korean government believes that South Korea is under constant threat of invasion from North Korea. Given this fact, South Korean leaders argue, it is important that South Korea remains strong and united. Political dissent and disunity, they claim, cannot be tolerated

*This is the same Woodrow Wilson who later became U.S. president and a strong human-rights advocate. Wilson taught government at Princeton before he entered politics.

because they might weaken South Korea and make it vulnerable to invasion from the north.

Many knowledgeable observers, however, both South Korean and foreign, dismiss this argument as the excuse of a repressive and authoritarian government that wants to keep itself in power. There is no real reason, they say, why South Korea could not become more democratic and free and still remain strong and united and able to defend itself should North Korea attack. The only thing standing in the way of greater democracy and liberty, they conclude, is a dictatorial government that refuses to change its ways.

The South Korean government has been charged with numerous instances of human-rights abuse, chiefly against workers who want better wages and the right to join labor unions, and against political dissidents. The following is a list of a few of the more outstanding cases of human-rights abuse in South Korea.

▪ In part, the enormous success of South Korean business and industry has been due to the low wages paid South Korean workers. The low wages mean that South Korean goods can sell cheaply on the world market because they will be less expensive than goods produced in countries where workers receive higher wages.

But when South Korean workers hold protest meetings to demand higher wages, government agents disrupt the meetings by beating up workers or by dumping buckets of human excrement on them. If the workers demand that the agents be charged with assault, the workers are charged with a crime and arrested while the agents go free. Government agents also work behind the scenes to convince employers to fire unruly workers or have them labeled as "communist agitators."

▪ The government prevents any political parties that advocate genuine democracy from having representation in the National Assembly. On numerous occasions, it has jailed opposition political leaders and subjected them to rigged trials, torture, and even death.

▪ In May 1980 a ten-day uprising against the government by the people of Kwangju in the Cholla district of South Korea was brutally put down. The government claims that fewer than two hundred lost their lives in the uprising. Unofficial estimates claim that the figure was closer to eight hundred or one thousand. As a result of the Kwangju uprising, Kim Dae Jung, a former presidential candidate and opposition leader was arrested, tried, convicted, and sentenced to death. Twenty-two of his followers were likewise arrested and sentenced to long prison terms.

■ South Korean newspaper editors are subject to arrest and detention for publishing articles that only mildly dissent from the government's position. Great encouragement is given to newspapers to print only news that puts the government in a good light. In 1983, for example, Kim Young Sam, a dissident leader, undertook a long hunger strike to dramatize his opposition to the regime. His fast was widely reported outside South Korea but within the country not one word was printed about it.

■ The KCIA (Korean Central Intelligence Agency), modeled on the American CIA, investigates and harasses Koreans living in South Korea. Koreans living in the United States have also been investigated and intimidated by KCIA agents. On several occasions, KCIA agents have kidnapped Koreans living abroad and brought them back to South Korea for trial and imprisonment.

Repression and human-rights abuse reached a peak in South Korea in the 1970s under President Park Chung Hee, a former general who was assassinated by the chief of the Korean CIA in 1979. The government, however, continues to be authoritarian and repressive.

American Policy Toward South Korea

For the first two decades following the Korean War, Washington remained silent about the failure of democracy in South Korea and its poor record on human rights. American officials publicly expressed hope that democracy was taking root in South Korea and praised that country's economic achievements. In practice, however, they tolerated South Korea's repressive measures and its authoritarian government.

For most Americans the failure of democracy was outweighed by the fact that the South Korean government was strongly anticommunist and a firm ally of the United States. Moreover, most Americans believed that however repressive and undemocratic the South Korean government was, it was a far better—and more desirable—government than the brutally repressive and totalitarian communist regime of North Korea.

During the human-rights upsurge of the 1970s, however, the American attitude toward South Korea began to change. The long involvement of the United States in the unpopular war in Vietnam caused many Americans to question America's support for nations that were regarded as oppressive and corrupt.

The first signs of official American dissatisfaction with South Korea came in 1972, when Representative Donald Fraser made South Korea a focal point of his subcommittee's investigation of human-rights abuse abroad. Fraser was an early leader of the human-rights campaign in Congress. Fraser and his subcommittee visited South Korea and interviewed victims of government repression. On one occasion, KCIA agents attempted to prevent Fraser from talking with former members of the National Assembly who were political dissidents by surrounding the homes of the dissidents. With the help of an official from the American embassy, however, Fraser broke through the human blockade and interviewed the dissidents.

On another occasion, Fraser talked with a former South Korean general who had been jailed and tortured by the KCIA for his opposition to the South Korean government. The interview so disgusted Fraser that afterwards he told the press that South Korea was now "not the country that American soldiers died for" in the Korean War. Fraser's subcommittee, however, did little more than document human-rights abuse in South Korea. Congress itself took no steps to penalize South Korea for its human-rights record.

After Jimmy Carter became president in 1977, relations between South Korea and the United States began to deteriorate. The South Korean government did not like Carter's strong human-rights program and had no idea what that program might mean for South Korea. The South Korean government was also in deep disagreement with Jimmy Carter's campaign promise to withdraw all American troops from South Korea in stages over several years. The South Koreans wanted the troops to stay.

The Carter administration, however, held back from any loud denunciation of human-rights abuse in South Korea. Instead it chose to work for the most part through channels of quiet diplomacy to let the South Korean government know that there was growing sentiment in Congress for a cutback in American aid and support for South Korea if the South Korean government failed to undertake democratic reforms.

The most dramatic point in Carter's relationship with South Korea came when Carter visited that country in mid-1979. Human-rights advocates in the administration warned the president not to go. A visit to South Korea, they said, would imply that Carter had given his approval to the South Korean government and would undermine his image as a strong supporter of human rights.

Carter, nevertheless, chose to go South Korea but only after his advisers had found a way to emphasize the administration's stand on human rights. Secretary of State Cyrus Vance, who traveled to South Korea with the president, quietly and secretly turned over a list of the names of over one hundred South Korean political prisoners about whom the U.S. government was concerned. Vance gave the list to the South Korean foreign minister and called for an investigation of each case. The Carter people then made the list public, in order to gain a response from the South Korean government. In a private conversation with South Korean president Park Chung Hee, Carter stated that the South Korean disregard for civil rights was undermining U.S. support for South Korea.

The American relationship with South Korea, however, sank to a new low in 1980 when the South Korean government arrested Kim Dae Jung. Kim was tried for treason for his part in the antigovernment Kwangju uprising and was sentenced to death. The United States joined nations around the world in condemning Kim's sentence as unjustified and cruel.

Were the Carter administration's human-rights efforts successful in South Korea? Only to a limited degree. The South Korean government did release a few political prisoners and downgraded the sentences of others. In January 1981, during Carter's last month in office, the South Korean government announced that Kim Dae Jung's death sentence had been commuted to life in prison. At the same time the prison sentences of several of Kim's followers were considerably shortened.

But the government has not abandoned its repressive policies. Chun Doo Hwan, who has been president of South Korea since 1980, has promised a "new politics" for South Korea, a politics that in his words would get South Korea out of "the rut of the old era." Chun has said that he wants a South Korea where several political parties can compete openly and without repression. He also wants South Korea to be rid of the mistakes and excesses of one-man, authoritarian rule.

Observers believe that it is still too early to say whether Chun is serious about his "new politics" and will reform South Korea or whether his program is nothing more than talk designed to improve South Korea's image abroad.

When it came to office in 1981, the Reagan administration

began to work to improve America's relationship with South Korea, a nation it regards as a "proven friend." Shortly after his inauguration, Reagan invited President Chun to Washington for talks. The South Korean leader was flattered that he was the first foreign head of state to meet with the new president.

Reagan confirmed America's commitment to South Korea and promised not to withdraw American troops from that country. He likewise promised that his administration would continue to supply full aid and assistance to South Korea and made no mention of South Korea's record on human rights.

Many observers, however, believe that the South Korean government must not read Reagan's public silence on human rights as permission to continue indefinitely to rule as they have been ruling. Change and reform, they say, must eventually come to South Korea for three reasons:

First, there are large numbers of South Koreans, perhaps a majority, that genuinely desire greater democracy. Almost all of South Korea's opposition leaders—whether they are now in jail in South Korea, in exile, or merely under government surveillance—are advocates of greater democracy and are deeply opposed to communism. The democratic opposition in South Korea must have meaningful political power and a voice in government affairs, the observers claim. Otherwise, a new, more militant and impatient generation may appear that will have nothing to do with the authoritarian tradition of the past and will blame the United States for keeping the older regime in power.

Second, South Korea must reform so that its image abroad will improve and so that it will receive greater international support. Among Americans, observers note, respect and esteem for South Korea has declined markedly since the Korean War. A 1980 Gallup Poll, for example, showed that only 38 percent of the Americans polled favored the U.S. defense of South Korea. Fifty percent opposed American military intervention even in the case of an invasion of South Korea by North Korea. Sixty-three percent regarded South Korea's record on human rights as poor.

If American support for South Korea has declined, the observers warn, that of other nations in the free world has fallen even lower. This low esteem does not bode well for South Korea's future, they claim, because South Korea needs international support—and especially American support—to continue to exist. And South Korea can only improve its image abroad and gain wider support if it undertakes true reform.

Finally, observers believe that South Korea must reform because it is in the American national interest for it to do so. It is awkward and at times embarrassing for the United States to be so closely tied to a nation so repressive and authoritarian. If the United States is genuinely to be the leader of the free world, observers argue, then the world that it leads must be genuinely free. If the United States is to be regarded as a champion of human rights and democracy, then its allies should be democratic and mindful of human rights—or at least be moving in that direction.

CHAPTER

8

HUMAN RIGHTS
AND THE
SOVIET UNION

The Soviet state's sixty-year history has been filled with horrible violence, hideous crimes at home and abroad, destruction, and the suffering, debasement, and corruption of millions of people. . . . A deeply cynical caste system has come into being, one which I consider dangerous (to itself as well as to all mankind). . . . beneath the petrified surface of our society exist cruelty on a mass scale, lawlessness, the absence of civil rights protecting the average man against the authorities, and the latter's total unaccountability toward their own people or the whole world. . . . As long as this situation continues, no one in our country, nor anyone in the world, can allow himself to lapse into complacency.

Soviet physicist
Andrei Sakharov in
Alarm & Hope (1978)

In theory, the Soviet Union upholds and espouses deeply humanitarian principles and basic human rights. In practice, however, it has proved to be one of the most repressive governments in history with a long record of human-rights abuse.

The Soviet Constitution of 1936, for example, guarantees "the citizens of the U.S.S.R." freedom of speech, of the press, of assembly, mass meetings, and street processions and demonstrations. It also guarantees a freedom of privacy of home and correspondence and a freedom from undue harassment by the government. Each of these basic human rights, however, is contradicted by another provision of Soviet Basic Law, which states that "the exercise of rights and liberties by citizens must not injure the interests of society and the state."

Soviet citizens cannot speak out against their government or engage in what is called "anti-Soviet behavior" without fear of arrest and punishment for criminal activity. Nor can they worship as they please, publish what they want to publish, or travel wherever they might want to travel, even within the confines of their own country.

Soviet human-rights abuse poses a difficult problem for American policymakers. Should the United States ignore Soviet human-rights violations so that the two superpowers can carry on discussions of primary concern to world peace such as arms control and limitations on nuclear weapons? Or should American leaders speak out against Soviet repression and brutality and risk angering the Soviet Union and causing it to withdraw from discussion and dialogue with the United States? This chapter will look at the Soviet record on human-rights abuse and how American foreign policy has dealt with that record.

The Soviet Union and
Human-Rights Abuse

Soviet human-rights abuse can be said to have begun in September 1918, when Vladimir Lenin, the Russian revolutionary leader, ordered his followers to "secure the Soviet Republic against class enemies by isolating them in concentration camps." Under Lenin, thousands of Soviet citizens were sent to concentration camps. The prisoners included members of all noncommunist political parties, priests, monks, nuns, and other religious people, students, intellectuals, and others.

Under Joseph Stalin, Lenin's successor, who emerged as head of the Soviet government in 1927, repression and human-rights violations grew more severe and more numerous. Stalin's government sent *millions* of Soviet citizens to concentration camps. Hundreds of thousands of these prisoners were used as workers in "forced labor" projects, building canals, roads, bridges, and other similar undertakings. They received no pay and were poorly fed and clothed. Many died from the hardships they experienced.

In addition, Stalin's government was responsible for the deaths of untold numbers of Soviet people. Estimates range from lows of between 15 million and 20 million to highs of 40 million and more. The great Russian writer Aleksandr Solzhenitsyn, after an exhaustive study of the subject, concluded that 60 million men and women had died as a result of Stalin's ruthlessness and repression.

Many died in the concentration camps. Others were executed by government agents, the secret police, or by army troops. Those executed included farmers who resisted collectivization;* members of rebellious minority nationalities, such as Ukrainians; and anyone who actively practiced their religion. The executed also included four hundred of the seven hundred generals of the Red Army; six members of the Politburo, the

---

*Stalin himself told Winston Churchill, the prime minister of Great Britain, that ten million *kulaks* had been killed by government agents or had died during the government's campaign against them. The *kulaks* were a class of prosperous Russian farmers who resisted the government's seizure of their property and the collectivization of Soviet farms.

governing committee of the Soviet Communist Party; and numerous other loyal communists who had fought in the Russian Revolution.

After Stalin's death in 1953, however, the large-scale executions and the mass consignments to concentration camps came to an end. Present-day Soviet leaders govern with a far milder hand than Stalin did and are far less likely to execute those regarded as enemies of the state. Nevertheless, the Soviet Union today remains a society where there is little freedom and little regard for human rights and dignity. Human-rights advocates have singled out three areas of serious concern: (1) the continued existence of forced labor projects; (2) Soviet treatment of Jews; and (3) the repression of dissidents.

(1) *Forced Labor Projects.* Many experts believe that the Sovet Union today uses the forced labor of political prisoners and others to build large projects in which paid labor would make costs prohibitive. A case in point is the construction of the oil pipeline from Siberia to Western Europe, a project that would help the Soviet economy by making Siberian oil available to the West, where it can be sold for hard Western currency.

(2) *The Treatment of Jews.* Soviet Jews who request emigration visas to leave the U.S.S.R. for Israel or elsewhere are either denied those visas or forced to pay enormous fees for them. The Soviet Jews who are denied exist visas are known as "refuseniks" and often pay heavily for their request to leave the Soviet Union. They may lose their jobs or be denied adequate housing or other social benefits of Soviet society. The Soviet treatment of Jews is in direct violation of the Helsinki Agreement, in which the Soviet Union and other signatory nations promised not to restrict the movement of people across national borders.

(3) *The Suppression of Dissidents.* Dissidents in the Soviet Union can be divided into three groups. There are *nationalist* dissidents—such as Lithuanians, Ukrainians, and others—who seek to preserve their national self-identity within the Soviet Union. There are *religious* dissidents—Russian Orthodox, Baptists, Pentecostalists, and others—who are harassed and intimidated by the government for practicing their religion. And there are *political* dissidents—men and women who oppose government policy and wish to reform the Soviet Union.

Soviet dissidents are dealt with under the law that defines all "anti-Soviet behavior" as criminal and face the possibility of one or more kinds of punishment. They may, for example, simply be arrested, tried, convicted, and sent to concentration camps, where they lose all contact with friends and relatives.

A second method of punishing dissidents is exile, either "external" or "internal." External exile means that the dissident is forced to leave the Soviet Union and move to another country. Notable examples of external exiles in recent years have been Aleksandr Solzhenitsyn, the writer, and Mstislav Rostropovich, the great cellist. Both Solzhenitsyn and Rostropovich now live in the United States.

Internal exile means that the dissident is sent to a Soviet city that is off limits to foreigners and where he or she can remain under constant surveillance by secret police and have little possibility of contact with former friends or relatives. The most famous internal exile in the Soviet Union today is Andrei Sakharov, a world-famous physicist and winner of the Nobel Peace Prize. Sakharov has been exiled to the city of Gorky for his work on behalf of human rights in the Soviet Union.

The third method used by the Soviet government to deal with dissidents is to send them to psychiatric hospitals. Viktor Fainberg was one Soviet dissident, among many, who was sent to a psychiatric hospital for "treatment." Rarely does the outside world hear about the activities of Soviet mental hospitals. But Fainberg's case proved an exception to that rule. Fainberg wrote down descriptions of his treatment on small pieces of paper, placed them in his mouth, and passed them to his wife when he kissed her during the once-a-month visits she was allowed to the hospital.

Fainberg's statement was circulated in the world press. In it he wrote of the "concentration of evil forces" occurring "under the fig-leaf of psychiatry" in the Soviet Union. He described the beatings he received in the hospital. He described being rolled up in wet bandages that were allowed to dry and contract, causing pain. He also told of sulfur injections that caused his temperature to rise to 104°F. Other dissidents have experienced similar and even harsher treatment in the psychiatric hospitals.

The dissident movement in the Soviet Union reached its peak in the 1960s and 1970s. During that period a number of prominent dissidents such as Andrei Sinyavsky and Aleksandr Ginzburg gained worldwide fame for their anti-Soviet views before being arrested, tried, and sent to concentration camps.

One of the most significant dissident groups was established in 1975 and called itself the "Public Group Furthering the Implementation of the Helsinki Agreement in the U.S.S.R." Also called the "Orlov Group, " for its leader Yuri Orlov, the group planned to monitor violations of human rights in the Soviet Union. The Orlov Group was the model for scores of other "Helsinki Watch Committees" that sprang up in the Soviet Union and in other communist countries after the Soviet Union signed the Helsinki Agreement and promised to respect human rights.

The dissidents of the 1960s and 1970s made their views known in *samizdat*, or clandestinely published and privately circulated articles and books. One important example of *samizdat* was the journal called *Chronicle of Current Events*, which gave its readers true stories of government repression and human-rights abuse in the Soviet Union. On its masthead, the *Chronicle* carried Article 19 of the United Nations Universal Declaration of Human Rights, which states that "everyone has the right of freedom of opinion and expression." During the late 1970s, however, the *Chronicle* ceased to appear after its editors were discovered and arrested.

During the late 1970s, the government was likewise able to suppress most other *samizdat* publications and to dissolve all of the Helsinki monitoring groups. Indeed, government suppression was so complete that today most Soviet dissidents are in concentration camps, in psychiatric hospitals, or in exile, and the dissident movement is largely a thing of the past.

American Foreign Policy and
Soviet Human-Rights Abuse

Two options are open to American foreign-policy makers in dealing with Soviet human-rights abuse. The first is to ignore that abuse or at least handle complaints about Soviet behavior privately through quiet diplomacy, so as not to embarrass or anger Soviet leaders. This has been the pattern followed by most American presidents. It has the virtue of keeping the lines of dialogue open between the two superpowers so that discussion on pressing issues such as arms control and nuclear weapons can be carried on.

The second option is to make human rights a part of America's Soviet policy. This was tried by the Congress in the mid-1970s, when the Jackson-Vanik amendment tied American-Soviet trade agreements to Soviet conduct on Jewish emigration. The Jackson-Vanik amendment so angered Soviet leaders that they immediately canceled a 1972 trade agreement and denounced American interference in Soviet affairs. The U.S. Congress, they said, had no right to tell the Soviet Union how it should handle its own internal matters.

President Jimmy Carter also attempted to tie human-rights issues to America's relationship with the Soviet Union. Carter and his advisers saw the human-rights cause as a way for the

United States to take what they called an "ideological offensive" against the U.S.S.R. By pressuring the Soviet Union on human-rights abuse, they believed, the United States could unmask Soviet repression and totalitarianism for the whole world to see. The United States, by contrast, would emerge as the champion of freedom and liberty.

The Carter administration particularly wanted to pressure the Soviet Union on the Helsinki Agreement. When it signed the Helsinki Agreement, the Carter people noted, the U.S.S.R. had agreed to respect the human rights of its citizens. And it had agreed to allow criticism of human-rights violations in the Soviet Union, when they occurred. The Helsinki Agreement had left the U.S.S.R. vulnerable to charges of human-rights abuse, the Carter administration concluded, and provided a means to work human-rights issues into America's relationship with the Soviet Union.

On February 5, 1977, two weeks after he took office, President Carter began to put his Soviet human-rights policy into practice by sending a letter to the world-famous Soviet dissident Andrei Sakharov. In the letter Carter declared his admiration for Sakharov and congratulated him on winning the Nobel Peace Prize. He also told the Soviet dissident that the Carter administration would seek "to promote respect for human rights not only in our country but also abroad."

Carter's letter to Sakharov was printed in newspapers throughtout the noncommunist world. It was the first time an American president had written to a Soviet dissident who still lived in the Soviet Union, and it was a symbolic gesture designed to underline U.S. support for the dissident movement.

Shortly after the Sakharov letter had made world news, Carter invited the exiled Soviet dissident Vladimir Bukovsky to the White House for a visit and conversation. Bukovsky had spent more than twelve years in Soviet prison camps and psychiatric hospitals for his writings and outspoken opinions. Like Sakharov, Bukovsky was a world-famous dissident whose cause had been taken up by human-rights advocates in America and Europe. He was widely regarded as a leading symbol of Soviet repression and injustice. Never before had an American president met with a Soviet dissident, and Bukovsky was a dissident of major stature.*

---

*One year before Carter took office, President Gerald Ford had refused to receive the exiled Russian writer Aleksandr Solzhenitsyn at the White House. Carter wanted his reception of Bukovsky to stand in contrast with Ford's refusal of Solzhenitsyn as a way of dramatizing the significance the Carter administration placed on human rights.

The letter to Sakharov and Bukovsky's White House visit deeply offended the Soviet Union, but it was the Sakharov letter that proved to be the deeper offense. In a letter to President Carter, Soviet leader Leonid Brezhnev expressed his strong distaste for Carter's human-rights campaign. The Soviet Union, Brezhnev declared, will not "allow interference in our internal affairs, whatever pseudo-humanitarian slogans are used to present it." Brezhnev chided Carter for his letter to Sakharov and called it "correspondence with a renegade who proclaimed himself an enemy of the Soviet state." The Soviet leader also warned Carter that the Soviet Union "would not like to have" its "patience tested in any matters of international policy, including the questions of Soviet-American relations."

In March 1977, one month after Brezhnev's letter, Secretary of State Cyrus Vance traveled to Moscow for negotiations with Soviet leaders. He carried with him a new arms-reduction package for Soviet consideration. Carter and his advisers had worked long and hard to develop the package and hoped that it would lead to a breakthrough in Soviet-American relations.

Soviet leaders, however, were of another mind. They declared the package totally unacceptable and rejected it outright. Moreover, they expressed deep displeasure with the manner in which the package was presented and displeasure with the Carter administration's attempts to break away from patterns of Soviet-American negotiations already established by previous American presidents.

Whether the Soviet rejection of the arms-control package was due to the Carter human-rights campaign or not, is not clear. Some observers believe that Soviet leaders rejected the package in order to "punish" Carter for the Sakharov letter and Bukovsky's White House visit. Others believe that the Soviet Union may have used its displeasure with the human-rights campaign as an excuse to cut off negotiations on an arms-reduction package that it had no real interest in. But whatever the reason, the rejection jolted President Carter, and it took his administration the better part of two years to restore dialogue with the Soviet Union.

Carter never again made use of a dramatic gesture such as the Sakharov letter or the Bukovsky visit to emphasize his opposition to human-rights abuse in the Soviet Union. He did not, for example, send a reply to a letter that Sakharov sent him later in his administration.

But Carter did not completely abandon his commitment to human rights. In every major speech he made on Soviet-American relations, he mentioned the importance of human rights and on two important occasions he made his views on human-rights abuse in the Soviet Union quietly but firmly clear to Soviet leaders.

The first of these occasions was the trial of Soviet dissident Anatoly Shcharansky. Shcharansky was a computer scientist and a Jew who had attmpted to get an exit visa to emigrate to Israel but had been refused. He was also a member of the Moscow Helsinki Watch Group. Shcharansky was unusually open and friendly with Western journalists in the Soviet Union, especially Robert Toth of the *Los Angeles Times*. In March 1977 Shcharansky was arrested and charged with spying for the CIA. His trial received worldwide attention.

President Carter quietly mentioned his concern for Shcharansky's fate in a private conversation with Soviet foreign mininster Andrei Gromyko. Gromyko was unmoved by Carter's concern and told the president that Shcharansky was "a microscopic dot who is of consequence to no one."

Protests against Shcharansky's arrest and trial and demands that the Soviet government be lenient came from around the world. But in July 1978 Shcharansky was convicted of espionage and sentenced to thirteen years' imprisonment.

President Carter's second exchange on human rights with a Soviet leader came in June 1979, at a summit conference with Soviet president Brezhnev in Vienna, Austria. Anticipating Carter's expression of concern for human rights, Brezhnev opened negotiations with a statement that excluded human rights as a topic of discussion. The Soviet Union, Brezhnev pointed out, does not base its relationship with the United States on problems that exist within American society. Soviet leaders, he explained, do not allude "to the unemployment rate in the United States, nor to racial discrimination, nor to violations of the rights of women" in the United States when they sit down to discuss matters with American leaders. "I want to talk about peace, and how to improve Soviet-American relations," Brezhnev concluded, "but human rights is a sensitive subject for us and is not a legitimate ground for discussion between you and me."

Later in the conference, however, President Carter brought up the question of human rights. "President Brezhnev," Carter said to the Soviet leader, "the subject of human rights is very important to us in shaping our attitude toward your country. You voluntarily signed the Helsinki accords," he continued, "which made this issue a proper item for state-to-state discussions." Carter pressed Brezhnev on Soviet dissidents and particularly on the case of Anatoly Shcharansky. He asked that the

Soviet government review the sentences of Shcharansky and other imprisoned dissidents, and perhaps lessen those sentences or allow the dissidents to leave the Soviet Union.

Brezhnev, however, was adamant. Shcharansky, he said, had been tried and convicted under Soviet law and it was his duty, as Soviet leader, to uphold Soviet law. Neither Shcharansky nor any other dissident would be allowed to go free.

Clearly, President Carter failed to pierce the intransigence of Soviet leaders on human-rights issues. But his human-rights policy should not be viewed as a complete failure in regard to the Soviet Union. It did have a few, but limited, successes.

Valentin Turchin, an exiled Soviet dissident, for example, believed that Carter made a difference because he brought Soviet human-rights abuse out into the open for the whole world to see. "Those less known suffer more," Turchin explained. By making the suffering and fate of Soviet dissidents a public cause, he went on, Carter had helped to give their lives and suffering meaning.

A second, limited success for human-rights policy during the Carter years was the weakening of restrictions on Soviet Jews who wished to leave the U.S.S.R. In weakening the restrictions, Soviet leaders were not bowing to Carter's pressure alone but to the worldwide outcry that followed the trial and conviction of Anatoly Shcharansky.

In 1976, 14,261 Jews had been allowed to leave the U.S.S.R. In 1977 that figure was 16,736. But in 1978, the year Shcharansky was convicted and sentenced, the number was 28,864, and in 1979 it shot up to 51,320. Since 1979, however, the number of Soviet Jews allowed to emigrate has fallen considerably. In 1981, for example, it was only 9,447. By 1983, it had dropped to 1,314.

Finally, the Carter administration was able to achieve a third and last success when it secured the release of five prominent Soviet dissidents from prison in exchange for two minor Soviet officials arrested in New York for espionage. The five included a Ukrainian nationalist, an Evangelical Baptist, and three leading Jewish dissidents. The five were taken from Soviet jails and prison camps, flown to New York City, and exchanged for the two Soviet spies.*

---

*It should be noted that the Soviet Union did not regard the release of the dissidents as a human-rights gesture, but as a simple exchange of prisoners convicted of serious crimes.

Carter, a Baptist by faith, later met personally with Geiorgy Vins, one of the released dissidents. Vins had been sentenced to prison and to internal exile in the Soviet Union for practicing his own Baptist faith. Soviet officials also allowed Vins's wife and five children to join him in the United States.

Each of the achievements of Carter's human-rights campaign was welcome and desirable. An impartial observer, however, must conclude that in the long run they did not amount to much. The Soviet Union today remains highly repressive and totalitarian. Indeed, Soviet dissidents noted that Soviet suppression of the dissident movement began to pick up after the Soviet Union signed the Helsinki Agreement. They likewise noted that after President Carter announced his human-rights policy, government repression grew even harsher. Dissidents began to be arrested in greater numbers, sentences grew more severe, and prison conditions for imprisoned dissidents markedly deteriorated.

In a statement highly critical of Carter's human-rights policy, former secretary of state Henry Kissinger declared that what the Carter policy proved above all was "the impotence of the United States" in attempting to influence or change Soviet behavior. The Carter policy, Kissinger claimed, had gained America nothing except worsened relations with the Soviet Union. Furthermore, he added, any human-rights policy directed against the Soviet Union will end in failure because Soviet leaders will not bow to foreign pressure and the Soviet Union is powerful enough to resist influence from abroad.

When he became president in 1981, Ronald Reagan quickly made it clear that he did not share Carter's hopes that the United States might influence the Soviet Union to improve its human-rights record. The communist nations, Reagan said at his first press conference, "reserve unto themselves the right to commit any crime, to lie, to cheat, in order to attain" their goals. "I think when you do business with them," he continued, "you keep that in mind."

Moreover, Reagan said, the only kind of morality the communists recognize is the morality that "will further their cause." Later in his administration, he referred to the Soviet Union as an "evil empire" that was the chief enemy of human freedom and liberty in the world today. Clearly, a president with this attitude toward the Soviet Union would not expect Soviet leaders to be sensitive about human-rights issues. For the Reagan administration, the best policy in *favor* of human rights was a policy *against* the U.S.S.R. and the communist world.

Carter's human-rights policy had gained the United States little in its relationship with the Soviet Union. What Reagan's tough, "hard line" policy will gain for America remains to be seen.

CHAPTER
9
HUMAN RIGHTS AND THE INTERNATIONAL ORGANIZATIONS

There is an inescapable link between respect for human rights and the maintenance of international peace and security, and no nation can justifiably claim immunity . . . from international scrutiny and expression of concern about flagrant and systematic abuses of the human rights of its citizens.

Kurt Waldheim
secretary general of the
United Nations, 1978

A merican foreign policy does not need to approach human-rights issues single-handedly. There are international organizations designed to deal with human-rights abuse that can censure governments with poor records on human rights. Two of these international organizations are the United Nations and the Organization of American States. The United States belongs to both groups and has worked through both to further the cause of human freedom and dignity.

As we shall see in this chapter, however, both the U.N. and the O.A.S. have problems that prevent them from being truly effective in the pursuit of human rights. The U.N. is deeply and vociferously anti-American. The O.A.S. is too weak. The question for American policymakers therefore becomes what can the United States do to improve and strengthen these organizations so that they can become more effective tools in the pursuit of human rights from the American point of view.

The United Nations and Human Rights

One of the primary reasons for the creation of the United Nations was the furtherance of human rights. The U.N. Charter of 1945 spoke of the importance of "fundamental human rights." In 1948 the Declaration of Human Rights listed and defined those rights and freedoms the United Nations regarded as fundamental. They included civil and political rights, such as freedom of speech, press, and a fair trial. They also included social and economic rights, such as the right to employment and the choice of work, the right to an education and medical care, and the right to Protection and support in old age.

The Declaration of Human Rights asserted that these rights were "a common standard of achievement for all peoples and all nations." To oversee the implementation of these rights throughout the world, the United Nations has established, over the past forty years, a variety of agencies and commissions. Their names reveal their duties and responsibilities.

There are the U.N. Commission on Human Rights and the Economic and Social Council. There are the Sub-Commission on Prevention of Discrimination and Protection of Minorities, the Commission on the Status of Women, and many others. There are also the better-known agencies, such as the I.L.O. (International Labor Organization), UNESCO (the U.N. Educational, Scientific, and Cultural Organization), and UNICEF (originally the U.N. International Children's Emergency Fund; now the U.N. Children's Fund).

In addition to the agencies, the United Nations has produced a considerable body of international treaty law in the area of human rights. These laws include the Genocide Convention of 1948, the Supplementary Convention on the Abolition of Slavery of 1956, the Convention on the Abolition of Forced Labor of 1957, the International Convention on the Elimination of Racial Discrimination of 1965, and numerous others.

From the beginning, the United States has been deeply involved in the affairs of the United Nations. American diplomats were instrumental in drawing up the U.N. Charter and the Declaration of Human Rights. Eleanor Roosevelt, the widow of president Franklin Roosevelt, was the first chairperson of the U.N. Commission on Human Rights.

Moreover, in the years since the United Nations was founded, the United States has supplied far more money than any other member nation to the United Nations' budget and to the budgets of the various agencies. Without American support, the United Nations would be hard-pressed to carry out its programs or finance its numerous undertakings.

During the past four decades, the United Nations has accomplished much good work. UNICEF has helped to eradicate dangerous diseases, such as smallpox, and to feed millions of hungry children. Other U.N. agencies have helped to improve the status of women in various societies, distributed information on birth control, and provided funds for the education and training of young men and women in developing societies.

But there have been problems. Many U.N. agencies, such as

the Commission on Human Rights and others, have fallen far short of expectation. Agency procedures, for example, often prove cumbersome and unwieldy. Frequently it takes years to bring a case of human-rights abuse to the agency's attention. By the time the case is heard, it is too late to do anything about it. But the deepest and most distressing problem at the United Nations today—at least from the point of view of the United States—is its strong anti-Americanism and its deep hostility to American interests.

That hostility takes two forms. The first is direct anti-American statements and actions. U.N. resolutions and declarations over the past two decades have often denounced the United States by name for fostering "aggression" and for "collaboration" with racism. These resolutions and declarations are passed by an overwhelming majority of U.N. members.

The second form that anti-American hostility takes in the United Nations is support for left-wing and Marxist movements. On numerous occasions the United Nations has expressed strong approval of Marxist revolutionaries in Central America; of the Palestine Liberation Organization, a terrorist group; and of other similar organizations. According to Midge Decter, the director of the conservative Committee for the Free World, the United Nations "has been turned . . . into a center for the articulation of tyranny." U.N. Ambassador Jeane Kirkpatrick believes that the anti-American hostility at the United Nations has left America's positions in that organization "essentially impotent, without influence, heavily outvoted, and isolated." In recent years, for example, the United Nations has declared Israeli-American military collaboration as a major factor leading to unrest and conflict in the Middle East. No mention, however, has ever been made of the seven thousand Soviet troops and military advisers in Syria as a cause of unrest in that part of the world.

The impotence of the United States is also obvious when it comes to human-rights resolutions at the United Nations. The United States has never been able to place human-rights violations in the Soviet Union or other communist nations on the agenda of the General Assembly or of any of the specialized committees and agencies. As far as the United Nations is concerned, human-rights abuse does not exist in the communist world. But the General Assembly and the various agencies regularly vote on resolutions condemning human-rights abuse in nations friendly to the United States, such as Israel, El Salvador, and Guatemala.

One of the most controversial U.N. agencies, from the

American point of view, is UNESCO. In recent years, UNESCO, which is based in Paris, has become a platform for vitriolic denunciations of the United States and other Western nations. UNESCO propaganda blames the United States and its allies for causing most of the world's problems by their "imperialist" actions. UNESCO publications attack free enterprise and advocate socialism.

A UNESCO program, announced in 1983 and named the "new world information order," is directed against the free press by providing for tighter controls over journalists covering stories in third-world countries and the communist world. The new world information order, if implemented, would mean that journalists would have to submit their stories to UNESCO censors for approval before publication.

Every American president from Harry Truman to Jimmy Carter has supported the United Nations and has believed that the United Nations served a useful purpose. During the past ten years, however, there has been a marked erosion of support for the United Nations among the American people. A Gallup Poll taken in the late fall of 1983 showed that only 36 percent of the Americans polled regarded the U.N. as doing a "good job."

During the same period, there has been a marked rise in the number of Americans who believe that the United States should "get out" of the United Nations. Ambassador Jeane Kirkpatrick, however, believes that the U.S. should stay in—as long as the U.N. can be persuaded to tone down its anti-American rhetoric and become a more responsible organization.

Most former American ambassadors to the United Nations have chosen to ignore the anti-American rhetoric so commonplace in U.N. debates and resolutions. But Ambassador Kirkpatrick believes that each anti-American denunciation must be answered directly and with firmness.

In March 1983 Kirkpatrick told a congressional committee that much needed to be done to increase American influence at the United Nations. She recommended that the United States directly inform nations that receive American aid and yet engage in anti-Americanism at the United Nations that American aid will be cut off unless the United States receives their support.

Congress responded by freezing the American contribution to the U.N. budget for 1984 at the 1983 level. Congress also passed legislation requiring the president to review America's relationship with the United Nations each year to see what "benefits" are "derived by the United States from participation in the United Nations." The legislation also required that, in the future, the secretary of state would issue a report each year on the voting records of all U.N. members to see how closely each member follows America's voting record on U.N. resolutions and declarations.

Ambassador Kirkpatrick believes that there was some improvement in America's position at the United Nations during 1983. "I think we are in a stronger position," she declared in an interview. "We are getting blamed in less strident ways and on fewer issues than we did before, and I think there are more moderate and reasonable resolutions being proposed."

But Kirkpatrick believes that more still needs to be done, especially with regard to the U.N. stand on human rights. Above all, she wants the United Nations to be consistent in its statements on human rights. "We have argued for a single standard" on human-rights issues, she has said on a number of occasions, meaning that the United Nations must learn to judge a nation like Chile "by the same standards" it judges communist Cuba and must treat all nations "in comparable ways."

President Ronald Reagan firmly supports Kirkpatrick's "get tough" and hardline policy at the United Nations. At the beginning of 1984, in order to underline and emphasize that policy, the Reagan administration announced that the United States would no longer participate in UNESCO after January 1, 1985. Reagan accused UNESCO of being unreasonably and obsessively anti-American and of opposing a free press. He likewise declared that American funds, which comprise one-quarter (or $50 million) of UNESCO's budget, would be withdrawn and that American representatives would no longer participate in UNESCO.

Observers believe that it is unlikely that the Reagan administration will propose to pull the United States completely out of the United Nations. But it is likely that Reagan and Kirkpatrick will continue to pressure the United Nations to tone down the anti-American rhetoric and to adopt a more balanced view on human-rights abuse throughout the world.

The Organization of American States and Human Rights

The Organization of American States, made up of the nations of North and South America, has established the Inter-American Commission on Human Rights (IACHR). The IACHR is composed of seven persons who serve four-year terms on the commission and are appointed by the Permanent Council of the O.A.S. The seven members serve in their individual capacities and are not representatives of specific governments.

The IACHR has the following powers and duties:

(1) It investigates complaints of human-rights abuse made to the commission by individuals and complaints arising from other sources.

(2) It may ask the governments involved for information about the complaints.

(3) It may seek information about the complaints by visiting specific countries, but only if those countries permit the commission to visit.

(4) It may compile reports on human-rights records of O.A.S. member nations.

Many IACHR reports have been direct and to the point. They refer to the individuals involved, both victims and persecutors, by name. They describe in detail the type of torture used and quote directly from interviews with political prisoners and other victims of government repression.

One IACHR report was highly critical of Brazil's record on human rights and declared that the Brazilian government was guilty of "exceedingly grave violations of the right to life"—a reference to the murder and execution of Brazilian political dissidents by government agents.

In reference to Chile another IACHR report said, in 1976, that "the practice of arbitrary jailings and persecution and tortures continues" even though the Chilean government had issued decrees denying human-rights abuse "for the purpose of tranquilizing or confusing world opinion."

In spite of its strongly worded reports, however, the IACHR has no coercive power. It cannot bring a government accused of human-rights abuse before a court and issue reprimands or inflict punishment. It must simply rely on the publication of its reports to bring cases of human-rights violations to the attention of world opinion. Moreover, the IACHR has a staff of only five professional and four clerical employees. Covering two continents, with a budget that comprises less than one percent of the total O.A.S. budget, these nine people must investigate over two thousand complaints of human-rights abuse each year.

Other problems faced by the IACHR have been the hostility of several O.A.S. members and a confusion over the definition of human-rights abuse. O.A.S. members that have been charged with human-rights abuse in IACHR reports are understandably reluctant to support the commission and its work. Frequently, they refuse to allow IACHR staff members to investigate complaints of human-rights abuse within their borders. Or they claim that "emergency conditions" (such as the existence of terrorist bands or other subversive groups) require repressive measures and severe laws. In such instances it is unusual for the IACHR to investigate even the most blatant examples of human-rights abuse.

During the first fifteen years of its existence, the IACHR rarely had its reports read at O.A.S. meetings. The reports were simply accepted by the presiding officer and then shelved after the commission had been thanked for its work. That practice came to an end in 1976 at the O.A.S. meeting in Santiago, Chile. On that occasion, the IACHR report on human-rights abuse in Chile was read before the meeting, and the Organization of American States adopted a resolution that called on Chile to improve its human-rights performance.

Since that time, IACHR reports have frequently been read at O.A.S. meetings, but a new conflict has developed. At the meeting in Grenada in 1977, for example, the Organization of American States adopted one resolution, sponsored by the United States, that praised the IACHR for its work in promoting civil and political rights.

But a second resolution, offered by Colombia, was likewise adopted. This resolution concentrated on economic and social rights and stated that earlier stages of economic development had created "serious social tensions and a political climate that is not conducive to the necessary respect for and protection of human rights" in many American nations. It called upon the United States to take the lead in the improvement of the economies of the undeveloped nations of the Western Hemisphere and implied that the United States was largely to blame for the economic backwardness of Central and South American nations.

In 1976 the U.S. Congress voted $102,000 in special funds to help finance the work of the IACHR. The Carter administration also strongly backed the commission and believed that its role in O.A.S. affairs should be strengthened.

The Reagan administration, however, has played down America's commitment to the IACHR out of concern that its reports might anger or embarrass proven American friends such as Chile, Argentina, or Brazil. Many observers believe that this is a mistaken policy. Unlike the United Nations, they note, the IACHR has never been anti-American or strongly ideological. Its reports have been balanced, well researched, carefully worded, and objective. For this reason alone, they argue, the IACHR has served a useful purpose in the promotion of human rights and its work should be encouraged, rather than ignored or neglected.

CHAPTER
10
CONCLUSIONS

*Human rights is the soul of our foreign policy . . .
because human rights is the soul of our sense of
nationhood.*

President Jimmy Carter
December 6, 1978

*A consistent and single-minded invocation of the
"human rights" standard in making United States
foreign policy decisions would serve neither our
interests nor the cause of freedom.*

Ernest Lefever
foreign-policy expert
in *The New York Times*
January 24, 1977

W_{hat} conclusions can we
draw from this survey of human rights and American foreign
policy?

First, we can conclude that any nation that wants to mix
human rights and foreign policy must make many difficult and
complex decisions. It must decide which kind of human rights it
wants to emphasize (for there are genuine differences on just
what human rights are) and it must decide how it can persuade
other nations to be concerned about these rights. It must also
decide on the degree of pressure it wants to bring to bear on
other nations and if it wants to direct its human-rights campaign
against friend as well as foe, against powerful nations as well as
weak. These questions are so intricate and involved that they
would intimidate even the most seasoned foreign-policy expert.
Yet they are questions that must be faced before a human-rights
policy is put into effect.

Second, we must conclude that if a human-rights policy is to
be effective, it must be carried out from a position of power.
Zbigniew Brzezinski noted that the Carter human-rights policy
was most successful when it dealt with relatively weak and
dependent nations such as Peru and Chile. When confronted
with a powerful nation like the Soviet Union, however, it had
very few successes. The U.S.S.R. was strong enough to resist
American pressure.

Third, we must conclude that there are genuine and serious
differences of opinion on the *desirability* of a human-rights pol-

icy. George Kennan, one of the foremost American experts on foreign policy, for example, criticized the Carter policy because to him it smacked of a moral crusade in which the United States attempted to dictate policy to other nations from a position of moral superiority. Kennan believed that human rights and foreign policy should never be mixed together.

Denis Brogan, another foreign-policy expert, attacked the Carter human-rights policy because it believed in what Brogan called "the illusion of American omnipotence" and because it assumed that the United States could remold the world. Realism, Brogan maintained, tells us that it is impossible for the United States to influence other peoples to behave like Americans and to adopt American traditions and institutions. Other nations, he concluded, have their own traditions and institutions that cannot be changed at a moment's notice or at America's command.

Fourth, we must conclude that there are elements in a human-rights policy that are deeply revolutionary and subversive—perhaps too revolutionary to be mixed with foreign policy. A human-rights policy assumes that a repressive government can be influenced to change and become less repressive.

But this may well be a false assumption. Repressive governments abuse human rights because they believe it is in their interest to do so. They believe they must be repressive in order to stay in power and prevent the rise of a political opposition that might challenge that power. A genuine human-rights policy will therefore act to undermine and destabilize the government in power, while it gives encouragement to those out of power who seek to overthrow the repressive government.

The question for foreign-policy makers then becomes: Is the repressive government so bad that it deserves to fall and be replaced by another government? Are there political parties or groups within the nation strong enough to rise to power and rule more justly and with a greater concern for human rights than the former government? These were the questions the Carter administration failed to ask when the governments of General Somoza in Nicaragua and of the Shah in Iran were facing widespread opposition. As a result, both Nicaragua and Iran fell victim to governments that proved far more repressive than the governments they overthrew.

Last, we must conclude that however complex and difficult a human-rights policy may be, human-rights issues are likely to play an important role in foreign-policy considerations for many years to come. There are many signs that this is so.

- In a 1982 speech before the British Parliament, President Reagan proposed what he called "Project Democracy," to spread information about democratic institutions to third-world nations and to the communist world. In his 1984 State of the Union address to Congress he renewed this commitment. Reagan envisioned the United States and other democratic nations working together to help foster democracy in nations where it had begun to develop. He likewise wanted America and other democratic societies to make an effort to convince neutral nations that democracy is far more attractive than communism. Project Democracy was Reagan's human-rights policy. If carried through, it would commit the United States to the establishment of democracy throughout the world.

- In 1983 Peter Reddaway, a British specialist in Soviet politics, noted that there was strong evidence that Soviet violations of human rights had grown more severe in recent years and that a revival of Stalinism might well be taking place. Reddaway cited several cases where Soviet government agents had used severe and brutal forms of torture in dealing with political prisoners. Torture had been outlawed in the Soviet Union after the death of Stalin, Reddaway pointed out, and its revival now could only mean that the U.S.S.R. was becoming more repressive and totalitarian.

  Concern for Soviet human-rights abuse has recently caused several American organizations such as the National Center for Responsible Public Policy to call for enforcement of Section 407 of the Smoot-Hawley Tariff Act of 1930. Section 407 forbade the importation of foreign goods "manufactured wholly or in part by convict labor or slave labor." Anti-Soviet human-rights activists want Section 407 enforced against the Soviet Union. At least half of American imports from the U.S.S.R., valued at $138 million per year, the advocates claim, are produced by forced labor. Banning these goods from the United States markets, they argue, would go a long way toward showing the Soviet Union that human-rights abuse cannot be tolerated.

- The January 29, 1984, edition of the *Washington Post* carried the news that a human-rights debate was shaping up in Congress. The previous fall, the city council of the District of Columbia voted to remove all city government funds that had been invested in firms doing business with South Africa.

  The city council's action ran counter to the Reagan administration's policy of "constructive engagement" with South Africa.

Since Congress must review all legislation passed by the Washington, D.C., city council, it would have to confront the council's action on South Africa. "We're going to have a hell of a fight on the floor of the House," said Representative Stewart B. McKinney (Republican, Connecticut), the ranking minority member of the House District of Columbia Committee. "It's going to be messy."

■ Finally, the United States is likely to be involved with human-rights issues in the future because the problem of human rights will not simply disappear. In a world where information can be sent from one point to another almost instantaneously, it is impossible to hide completely all stories of government repression and human-rights abuse. Fifty or a hundred years ago, it was possible for a nation to adhere to the principle of noninterference and deny the right of any other nation to intervene in its internal affairs. Today that position is much less tenable.

Since World War II a body of international law and tradition has developed concerning the practice of human rights. America has played an important part in the development of that law and tradition, and it will be important that the United States continues to play a significant role in its development.

As we have seen in this book, the protection of human rights in the world today leaves much to be desired. There is still much work to be done and many problems to be ironed out. The question for Americans to ask themselves is, Can the United States afford to turn its back on the development of human rights, or should it make its influence felt in the development of those rights?

BIBLIOGRAPHY

*An asterisk (*) denotes a book of
special interest to younger readers.*

The liberal point of view on human rights and foreign policy is presented in Sandy Vogelgesang, *American Dream–Global Nightmare: The Dilemma of U.S. Human Rights Policy** (New York: W. W. Norton, 1980). Vogelgesang was a member of the State Department planning staffs for both Henry Kissinger and Cyrus Vance. For the conservative point of view, see Howard Wiarda, ed., *Human Rights and U.S. Human Rights Policy** (Washington, D.C.: American Enterprise Institute, 1983). This book contains essays by six prominent conservative writers.

For the complete texts of the major U.N. human-rights documents, see Paul Williams, ed., *The International Bill of Human Rights** (Glen Ellen, Calif.: Entwhistle Books, 1981). For a very detailed discussion of the human-rights issue, see Donald Kommers and Gilburt Loescher, eds., *Human Rights and American Foreign Policy* (Notre Dame, Ind.: University of Notre Dame Press, 1979).

Former President Jimmy Carter discusses his human-rights policy at length in his memoirs, *Keeping Faith* (New York: Bantam, 1982). On the Carter administration, also see Cyrus Vance, *Hard Choices: Critical Years in America's Foreign Policy* (New York: Simon and Schuster, 1983). Zbigniew Brzezinski's *Power and Principle: Memoirs of the National Security Adviser, 1977–1981* (New York: Farrar Straus Giroux, 1983), is excellent on the difficulties of developing an adequate human-rights policy.

One of the best books on President Ronald Reagan is Lou Cannon's *Reagan* (New York: G. P. Putnam's Sons, 1982). For Ambassador Jeane Kirkpatrick's views, see her *Dictatorships and Double Standards: Rationalism and Reason in Politics* (New York: American Enterprise Institute/Simon and Schuster, 1982).

An excellent guide to South Africa is found in Harold Nelson, ed., *South Africa, A Country Study** (Washington, D.C.: American University, Foreign Area Studies, 1981). On American relations with South Africa, see the report of the Study Commission on U.S. Policy Toward Southern Africa, *South Africa: Time Running Out** (Berkeley, Calif.: University of California Press, 1981). Also very helpful is Robert Rotberg, *Suffer the Future: Policy Choices in Southern Africa** (Cambridge, Mass.: Harvard University Press, 1980).

On South Korea, see Frederica M. Bunge, *South Korea, A Country Study** (Washington, D.C.: American University, Foreign Area Studies, 1982). Slightly dated but still very good is Frank Baldwin, ed., *Without Parallel: The American-Korean Relationship Since 1945** (New York: Pantheon Books, 1974).

The classic study of human rights and repression in the Soviet Union is Aleksandr I. Solzhenitsyn, *The Gulag Archipelago** (New York: Harper & Row, 1973–75). This book is three volumes long, but it tells in vivid detail the violations of human freedom and dignity committed by the U.S.S.R. It is one of the most important books of our time.

The use of psychiatry by the Soviet Union to repress the dissident movement is discussed in Zhores A. Medvedev and Roy A. Medvedev, *A Question of Madness: Repression by Psychiatry in the Soviet Union** (New York: W. W. Norton, 1971). On Soviet repression, see also Andrei D. Sakharov, *Alarm and Hope** (New York: Alfred A. Knopf, 1978). This is a collection of Sakharov's most important writings and comments on human rights. It contains his controversial correspondence with President Jimmy Carter and the speech he prepared for delivery at the 1975 Nobel Prize awards ceremony. Soviet officials refused to allow Sakharov to leave the U.S.S.R., and the speech "Peace, Progress, and Human Rights" was read in Stockholm by his wife, Elena Bonner.

INDEX

Adams, John Quincy, 51–52
Afghanistan, Soviet invasion
  of, 32–33
AFL-CIO. *See* American Federation of Labor and Congress of Industrial Organizations
Africa
  Carter's policy, 31, 67–68
  Reagan's policy, 44
  Soviet influence in, 44, 64
  see also specific countries
African Development Fund, 19
Afrikaans, 66
American Federation of Labor and Congress of Industrial Organizations (AFL-CIO), 18
Amin, Idi, 20
Amnesty International, 1–2, 18
Anti-Apartheid Conference (1977), 67
Anti-Sandinistas, 43
Anti-Soviet behavior, 83, 85

Apartheid, 63–66
  U.S. opposition to, 66–70
Argentina, 19–20, 41
  Carter's policy, 31
  Reagan's policy, 43
Arms control negotiations (U.S.-U.S.S.R.), 89
Arms sales, 29, 67. *See also* Military aid
Assembly, freedom of, 7
Authoritarian societies, 41

Banning, in South Africa, 65–66
Between Two Ages (Brzezinski), 26
Biko, Stephen, 66, 68
Bill of Rights (England), 8
Bill of Rights (U.S.), 7
Bishop, Maurice, 44–45
Blaine, James G., 53
B'nai B'rith International, 18
Borah, William, 55
Brademas, John, 22
Brazil, 102
Brezhnev, Leonid, 89–91
Bricker, John, 57

Brogan, Denis, 108
Brzezinski, Zbigniew, 6, 26–28, 31–32, 107
Bukovsky, Vladimir, 88–89
Bureau of Human Rights and Humanitarian Affairs (U.S. State Department), 21, 28

Cambodia. *See* Kampuchea
Carter, Jimmy, 23–33, 49, 58–59, 106, 108
  Inter-American Commission on Human Rights, 103
  Kirkpatrick, Jeane, criticism of, 38–42
  Reagan's attitude toward, 37–38
  South Africa, 67–68
  South Korea, 77–78
  Soviet Union, 87–93
  United Nations, 100
Censorship
  South Africa, 65
  South Korea, 76
  Soviet Union, 83
Central Intelligence Agency (CIA), 43
Chile, 19–21, 107
  Carter's policy, 29, 31
  Inter-American Commission on Human Rights, 102–103
  Reagan's policy, 43
China, 30
Christopher, Warren, 29
Chronicle of Current Events (*samizdat* journal), 87
Chun Doo Hwan, 78–79
CIA. *See* Central Intelligence Agency
Civil and political rights, 7–10
  in Carter's Presidential Directive 30, 28

in U. N. Declaration of Human Rights, 97
  in Vance's speech on human rights, 27
Civil and Political Rights, U.N. Covenant on, 56–57
Civil Rights Act of 1964, 17
Clay, Henry, 51
Cold War, 58
Colombia, 103
Commentary (periodical), 39
Commission on Human Rights, U.N., 98–99
Commission on the Status of Women, U.N., 98
Communism
  Reagan administration's view of, 45
  U.S. relations with communist countries, 57–58
Conference of East Caribbean Nations, 44
Congress, U.S., 15–22, 87
  District of Columbia's human rights action, 109–110
  Inter-American Commission on Human Rights, funding of, 103
  United Nations, 100–101
Constitution, American, 7–8
Constructive engagement, 69
Convention on the Abolition of Forced Labor, U.N., 98
Convention on the Prevention and Punishment of the Crime of Genocide, U.N., 57, 98
Convict labor. *See* Forced labor
Covenant on Civil and Political Rights, U.N., 56–57
Covenant on Economic, Social, and Cultural Rights, U.N., 57

Cruel and unusual punishments, 7
Cuba, 40, 44

Declaration of Human Rights, U.N. *See* Universal Declaration of Human Rights
Declaration of Independence, 7
Declaration of the Rights of Man and of the Citizen (France), 8
Decter, Midge, 99
Democracy, 9–10
    Project Democracy, 109
Developing nations. *See* Third World
Dissidents, political, 29
    South Africa, 65
    South Korea, 74–77
    Soviet Union, 85–92
District of Columbia, 109–10
Due process, 7

Economic and Social Council, U.N., 98
Economic rights. *See* Social and economic rights
Economic, Social, and Cultural Rights, U.N. Covenant on, 57
Education, 2, 8, 98
Elderly, rights of, 98
El Salvador, 99
Employment, 8, 98
England. *See* United Kingdom
Exile, as punishment in Soviet Union, 86
Export-Import Bank, 43, 67

Fainberg, Viktor, 86
Fear, freedom from, 56
Federation of American Scientists, 18
Forced labor, 109
    Soviet Union, 84–85

Forced Labor, U.N. Convention on the Abolition of, 98
Ford, Gerald, 88
Foreign aid
    human-rights record as basis of, 18–20, 22, 28–29
    Reagan's policy, 43
    South Korea, 74
Foreign Assistance Act of 1973, 19
Foreign policy
    Brzezinski's view of, 26
    Carter's policy, 23–33
    Congressional involvement, 17–22
    history of United States human rights and, 49–59
    human rights as subject of, 10–14, 107–108
    Reagan's policy, 35–45
    United States-South African relations, 63–64, 66–70
    United States-South Korean relations, 73, 76–80
    United States-Soviet relations, 83–84, 87–93
Founding Fathers, American, 49–50
Four freedoms speech (F. D. Roosevelt), 55–56
France, 8
Franklin, Benjamin, 50
Fraser, Donald, 6, 17–18, 21, 77
Freedom of assembly, press, etc. *See* Assembly, freedom of; Press, freedom of the; etc.
Freedoms, four. *See* Four freedoms speech
French Revolution, 50

Gallatin, Albert, 49–50
Gaspari, Elio, 30
Genocide convention, U.N.,
57, 98
German Constitution (1919),
8
Germany, Federal Republic of
(West Germany), 32
Ginzburg, Aleksandr, 86
Global Issues Cluster, 28
Government repression, 2, 7,
12, 14, 108
Carter's policy, 28
South Africa. *See* Apart-
heid
South Korea, 74–77
Soviet Union, 83–84,
92
Great Britain. *See* United
Kingdom
Greece, 51
Grenada, 32
U.S. invasion, 44–45
Gromyko, Andrei, 90
Guatemala, 99
Guinea, 29

Harkin amendment, 19–20
Harkin, Tom, 16, 19, 22
Hawk, David, 30
Helsinki Final Act (Helsinki
accords), 11, 13, 85, 88, 90,
92
Helsinki Watch Committees,
86–87, 90
Honduras, 43
House of Representatives,
U.S., 18, 77. *See also* Con-
gress, U.S.
Human rights
American history, 47–59
Amnesty International
report, 1–2
Carter's policy, 23–33,
49, 58–59

Congressional concern
with, 15–22
foreign policy and, 10–
14, 107–108
international organiza-
tions, 95–103
Kirkpatrick, Jeane, thought
and writings of, 38–42
Reagan's policy, 37–38,
42–45
South Africa, 61–70
South Korea, 71–80
Soviet Union, 81–93, 109
two categories, 7–10
Human Rights, U.N. Com-
mission on, 98–99
*Human Rights in the World
Community: A Call for U.S.
Leadership* (House subcom-
mittee report), 18
Humphrey, Hubert, 16
Hunger, 2, 8

IACHR. *See* Inter-American
Commission on Human
Rights
Illiteracy, 2
I.L.O. *See* International Labor
Organization
Indonesia, 29, 31
Inter-Agency Group on Hu-
man Rights and Foreign
Assistance (U.S. State De-
partment), 28–29
Inter-American Commission
on Human Rights (IACHR),
101–103
Inter-American Development
Bank, 19
International Convention on
the Elimination of Racial
Discrimination, U.N., 98
International Development
and Food Assistance Act,
19–20

International Labor Organization (I.L.O.), 98
International law, 98, 110
International League for Human Rights, 18
International organizations, 95–103. *See also* League of Nations; Organization of American States; United Nations
Iran, 29–30, 32, 38–42, 108
Isolationism, 50
Israel, 99
Italian immigrants, attacks on (in 1880s and 1890s), 53
Italy, 53

Jackson-Vanik amendment, 20, 87
Jacobson, Dan, 62
Jamaica, 43–44
Japan, 8
Jews, Soviet, 20, 85, 91
Job, right to, 8, 98
Jury, trial by, 7

Kampuchea, 1
Kassebaum, Nancy, 69–70
KCIA. *See* Korean Central Intelligence Agency
Kennan, George, 108
Kennedy, John F., 58, 67
Kim Dae Jung, 76, 78
Kim Young Sam, 76
Kirkpatrick, Jeane, 38–42, 45, 99–101
Kissinger, Henry, 17, 21, 68, 92
Korea, Republic of (South Korea), 13, 29, 71–80
Korean Central Intelligence Agency (KCIA), 76–77
Korean War, 74
Kulaks, 84

Kwangju uprising, South Korea, 75–76, 78

Labor
forced, 84–85, 98, 109
South Africa, 67–68
South Korea, 75
Latin America, 51–52, 58. *See also* specific countries
League of Nations, 55
Lefever, Ernest, 106
Left-wing revolutionary governments, 41–42
Lenin, Vladimir, 84
Liberia, 68
Life, liberty, and the pursuit of happiness, 7
Lobbying groups, 18

Machel, Samora, 44
McKinley, William, 54
McKinney, Stewart B., 110
MacLeish, Archibald, 48
Magna Carta, 8
Malnutrition, 2
Manley, Michael, 43–44
Marcos, Ferdinand, 72
Medical care, 2, 8, 98
Meskito Indians, 43
Mexico, 8
Middle East conflict, 99
Military aid, 20, 29, 43
Minorities, U.N. Sub-Commission on Prevention of Discrimination and Protection of, 98
Mondale, Walter, 67
Monroe Doctrine, 51–53
Monroe, James, 51–52
Morality and Foreign Policy (essays), 39
Mozambique, 44

National Center for Responsible Public Policy, 109

National Council of
Churches, 18
National dissidents, Soviet
Union, 85
National Security Council, 28
Neutrality, 50
New Orleans anti-Italian riot
(1891), 53
New world information or-
der, 100
Nicaragua, 108
Carter's policy, 29–30, 32
Kirkpatrick, Jeane, criti-
cism of Carter, 39–42
Reagan's policy, 42–43
Nigeria, 68
Nixon, Richard M., 17
Nonintervention, 13, 52–53,
110
Nuclear weapon stockpiles, 57
Nutrition, 8
Nyerere, Julius, 62

Organization of American
States (O.A.S.), 21, 45, 97,
101–103
Orlov Group, 86

Pahlavi, Mohammed Reza,
Shah, 29–30, 38
Panama Canal Treaty, 30–31
Paraguay, 29
Park Chung Hee, 76, 78
Peru, 31, 107
Petition of Right (England), 8
Philippines, 13, 29, 54
Pinochet, Augusto, 31
Political dissidents (group of
Soviet dissidents), 85
Political prisoners, 2
Carter's policy, 30–31
South Africa, 65–66
South Korea, 75–76, 78
Soviet Union, 84–87, 90–
91

Political rights. *See* Civil and
political rights
Portugal, 41
Poverty, 2, 8
Power and Principle (Brzezins-
ki), 31
Presidential Directive 30
(Carter 1978), 28
Press, freedom of the, 7, 97
new world information
order, 100
South Africa, 65
South Korea, 76
Soviet Union, 83
Prisoners, exchange of, 91
Prisoners, political. *See* Politi-
cal prisoners
Private investment, 43
Project Democracy, 109
Psychiatric hospitals, commit-
ment of Soviet dissidents
to, 86–87
Public Group Furthering the
Implementation of the Hel-
sinki Agreement in the
U.S.S.R., 86
Public office, right to hold, 8
Punishment. *See* Banning;
Cruel and unusual punish-
ments; Exile; Political pris-
oners; Torture

Racial discrimination, in
South Africa. *See* Apartheid
Racial Discrimination, Inter-
national Convention on the
Elimination of, 98
Reagan, Ronald, 33, 35–45,
49, 58–59
Inter-American Commis-
sion on Human Rights,
103
Project Democracy, 109
South Africa, 68–69
South Korea, 78–79

Taft, William Howard, 54
Thailand, 29
Third-world countries, 9–10, 58
Timerman, Jacobo, 31
Torture, 2
  South Africa, 66
  South Korea, 75, 77
  Soviet Union, 86, 109
Trade restrictions, for control of human-rights abuses, 20, 109
  Rhodesia, 67
  South Africa, 67–68
  Soviet Union, 87
Travel restrictions, Soviet Union, 83, 85
Trials, 7, 97
Truman, Harry S., 56, 100
Turchin, Valentin, 91

Uganda, 19–20
U.N. See United Nations
UNESCO. See United Nations Educational, Scientific, and Cultural Organization
UNICEF. See United Nations Children's Fund
Union of Soviet Socialist Republics, 8, 13, 19–20, 29, 37, 57–58, 81–93, 107, 109
  Afghanistan invasion, 32–33
  Africa, influence in, 44, 64
  Jews, restrictions on, 20, 54, 85, 91
  United Nations, 99
United Kingdom, 8, 32
United Nations (U.N.), 13, 45, 56–57, 67, 97–101. See also Universal Declaration of Human Rights
United Nations Children's Fund (UNICEF), 98

United Nations Educational, Scientific, and Cultural Organization (UNESCO), 98, 100–101
United States
  Constitution, 7–8
  Grenada invasion, 44–45
  human rights in American history, 47–59
  Organization of American States, 103
  United Nations, 98–101
  see also Congress, U.S.; Foreign policy; and names of specific presidents
Universal Declaration of Human Rights, U.N., 1, 11, 13, 56–57, 87, 97–98
Uruguay, 19–20, 43
U.S.S.R. See Union of Soviet Socialist Republics

Vance, Cyrus, 27–28, 48, 78, 89
Vins, Geiorgy, 92
Vorster, B. J., 67–68
Voting rights, 8

Waldheim, Kurt, 96
Want, freedom from, 56
Washington, George, 50
West Germany. See Germany, Federal Republic of
Wilson, Woodrow, 54–55, 74
Women, U.N. Commission on the Status of, 98
Woods, Donald, 66
World War I, 55

Young, Andrew, 31, 67

Zimbabwe, 9, 30–31, 68
Zvobgo, Eddison, 9–10